PATENT FOR MURDER

RICHARD B. ROSSI

Based in part on a true story with real characters. Additional characters have been composited or invented, and a number of incidents fictionalized.

Library of Congress Control Number: 2012903104
Printed by CreatsSpace, North Charleston, SC

DEDICATION

To Giuseppe and Vicenza Rossi, Henry and Rosilda Beron, and all of their descendants. May their lives be remembered by many and their accomplishments be known by all.

CONTENTS

ACKNOWLEDGMENTS

Special thank you to my wife, Janet, and children, Alecia and Aaron, who have afforded me the seemingly countless hours of time and space to be creative.

For their assistance and contributions to this book, the author is particularly grateful to Rita (Beron) Rossi, Delia (Rossi) Mailloux, Jerry T. Rossi, Lawrence, Susan, and Sandra Rossi, Nicholas Rossi, Alecia Rossi Ojinaga, Aaron John Rossi, Joseph Rossi, Kevin Rossi, Brittney Weisman, Joanna Spagnolini, and Daniel Phillips, cover artist.

For their continued support, the author would also like to thank the Peter Ojinaga family, Raymond and Delia Mailloux family, Jerry T. and Marie Rossi family, Pete and Martha Mantaian Family, George and Jean Mantaian family, Christopher and Diana Miner family, William and Carol Hull family, Manuel G. Perez, Arthur Morris, Dennis Garrison, James Caparelli, Kevin Pirrello, Ryan Alvord, Jeremy Neel, and Biscuit, Sophia, and FiFi.

PREFACE

In the early nineteen hundreds, experimentation with the aviation concept of unmanned remote controlled flying weapons was on the forefront of the development of weapons technology by several countries. For example, in 1914 the British conducted tests with a radio-controlled "flying bomb." However, failed attempts to successfully launch the device caused the project to be discontinued.

In the United States during the same time period, notably *three men* worked vigorously on the same aviation concept in three separate situations unbeknownst to each other. Two of these men were highly educated, successful engineers, who each ultimately received government funding to continue their pioneering research with unmanned flying bombs for the military. These two well-known men later went on to be corporate business owners leaving their mark on US history.

The third man was an Italian immigrant, a naturalized citizen of the United States, who had little formal education, no financial backing, and no special tools or equipment. Having served in the Italian Army during World War I, he conceived an idea of an unmanned flying torpedo, constructed it, successfully test-flew it, and patented it in Washington, DC.

This man was my grandfather. He too was a pioneer of the military technology widely used today to save American lives. His name, his accomplishments, and his flying aerial torpedo device went unpublished and unknown to anyone alive today. It became my quest to find out why.

1 THE DISCOVERY

I remember when I was about six years old, I would snoop through my parents' bedroom looking for hidden treasures. Back then, in 1961, my parents owned a three-piece metal bedroom set in a wood-grained finish. The bureau and dresser had large, round brass handles that my mother would keep neatly polished. In the corner of the room was a built-in bookcase with six-panel glass doors on top and three drawers with brass pull handles at the bottom. Mom kept important bills and paperwork there—in the bookcase drawers. Moreover, that was where I started my searches every time.

Mom's dresser usually only contained clothes, but occasionally I would find a piece of bubble gum or candy on the bottom of a drawer—God only knows why she kept them there. Dad had a Knapp shoebox in the top drawer of his bureau where he kept things he liked close by. His metal-cased tape measure and a metal Ray-O-Vac flashlight were in the box, as well as a Brown and Sharpe micrometer in its own case that Dad used at work and some pocket change. My father covered all that up with his socks and underwear.

One day while shuffling around through Dad's top drawer, I discovered something new. Under the shoebox was a thick black book—very intriguing for a young explorer.

I removed it from the drawer and set it on the bed. The book's cover was black and textured, bound by a shoestring-type rope and tied into a bow. The pages of the book were thick and black. In the book, I found old photographs neatly placed on each page. Little white corner keepers glued to the page kept each picture in place. Flipping through, I realized that I did not recognize most of the people in the pictures.

My mother came into the room at this point and asked me what I had found. Knowing I should not have been looking through their dressers, I reluctantly showed her the mysterious photo album. She sat on the bed near me and began to explain each person in the pictures. These were actually pictures of my parents, grandparents, aunts, uncles, and nephews as well as my older brother Jerry and older sister Delia. When we reached the last page of the photo album, we saw an old newspaper clipping glued to the inside. On this clipping were some pictures of another man that I did not recognize and two pictures of something that looked like a small airplane. Of all the pictures, these piqued my interest the most. I asked my mother about the clipping and pictures.

Pointing to the clipping, she told me that my dad's father, my grandfather, was an inventor. His name was Giuseppe Rossi.

It sounded interesting, but I was not exactly sure what an "inventor" was. She explained to me that my grandfather had designed the little plane in the picture I was looking at.

"Did he fly in it?" I asked.

"No," she said. "It was too small, and it flew by itself. It was a…robot plane."

After all these years of searching through my dad's sock drawer, I had finally found the type of hidden treasure I had been seeking—a robot plane!

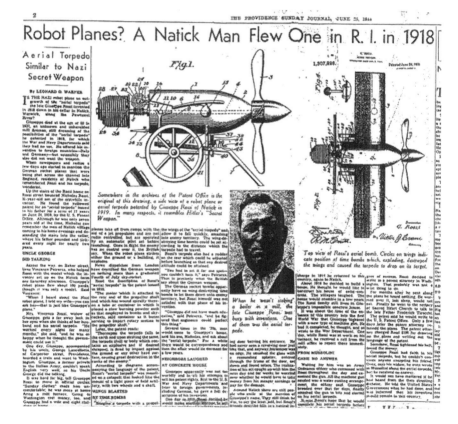

2 SHOW AND TELL

At the time of my new discovery, I was in the first grade at Maisie E. Quinn Elementary School in West Warwick, Rhode Island. I could hear and see my school from our front porch. This particular month was "show and tell" at school. Of course, I wanted to bring in the robot plane article and show my friends how smart my grandfather was, but my mom said no. She was afraid I would lose some of the pictures in the photo album. I suspected she was willing to negotiate, though, and—lucky for me—she was this time.

She asked me which of the pictures from the album I wanted to take to school. Mom thought for a second, untied the photo album, and then handed me the back cover with the newspaper clipping on it. She told me to be careful and bring it straight home after school. I was excited and agreed.

The next day at show and tell, I could hardly contain myself. I could not wait to show the others what I'd found. One boy got in front of the classroom and showed his new baseball glove, and a girl showed her favorite doll. Then it was my turn.

I stood at the front of the class and held up the photo album cover with the newspaper clipping on it. I explained to the class, "This is a story about my grandfather. He built this robot plane." Some of my classmates, mostly the girls, tuned out immediately, but the boys and Mrs. Leighton were very interested.

Robots were just starting to become popular on television programs and in comics. After the album cover was passed around the classroom and everyone had gotten a look at the pictures, the teacher read the article to herself at her desk. Later she commented on how interesting she thought it was and asked if my grandfather had become famous from his invention. I had no clue.

That evening after dinner, I told my dad how I had taken the newspaper clipping written about his father to school. My father was surprised. (I guess my mom could keep a secret from Dad.)

3

"What did your teacher think of it?" he inquired.

"My teacher wants to know if your father ever became famous. What does that mean?" I asked him.

"I think she wants to know if he made a lot of money from his invention. The answer is no, sadly, not a penny."

"Why not?"

"Because a man in Massachusetts invented a *rocket*-powered plane. It was faster and better."

My father was referring to Robert Hutchings Goddard, rocketry and space flight pioneer, though I did not know it at the time.

Years passed from elementary school through high school, and I found every imaginable reason to take my grandfather's story to school. Classroom studies and discussions about World War I, World War II, and Vietnam always provided an opportunity to bring up his patented invention. With the help of my history classes, I was beginning to understand the full implications of my grandfather's work.

The robot plane was actually a mighty war machine that could fly, drop from the sky, and—without warning—kill people and destroy property. He had essentially created a *weapon of mass destruction*. My grandfather, Giuseppe Rossi, had created an instrument of war and devastation that could have changed American military and world history. However, it had not. No one had ever spoken of this device, and besides my relatives, no one knew anything about Giuseppe Rossi. I was curious as to why.

The more I learned, the more questions I had and the more I wanted to know about my grandfather the inventor, the machine he'd made, and what came of it all. My overwhelming curiosity as to why my grandfather had not made it into the history books and why there was never a History Channel special about the robot plane had motivated me to search for some answers. I began my search with the only piece of information I had available to me—the old newspaper article from the family photo album.

My research taught me so much about my family's past, and I have learned of relatives I never knew existed. I also gained insight into life in the early nineteen hundreds and how being Italian, French, or Portuguese determined where you would live, work, and whether you were prosperous or not. Furthermore, I learned about others who had designed and implemented aerial bombs and the havoc these weapons created in the past. The early models for aerial weaponry are still used today for modern devices and for developing new warfare technology. Gathering information for this book has been slow and tedious, but interesting and exciting as well. And because I live in California now, it has been difficult locating records of my family history in Rhode Island—but this has been half the challenge.

I have studied military history and world history trying to find out more about my grandfather's robot plane invention. I eventually learned that he had patented his invention and had built a prototype—a working model. This, of course, led to even more questions.

Where was that original machine? Why had he not become famous? How was he able to construct such a device with limited funds, no formal engineering education or experience, and using only basic hand tools?

My curiosity was becoming an obsession.

3 FORNELLI, ITALY

It was a crisp October afternoon in the small mountaintop village of Fornelli, Italy. Nearly two hours from the bustling, populated city of Campobasso, Fornelli was a quaint, sleepy town surrounded by medieval walls in a rural area lush with olive trees. Augustino Rossi was tending to his pig farm when a neighbor summoned him and advised him to go home immediately. Augustino dropped what he was doing and ran to his small stone house.

Getting closer, he heard a woman's sharp cries and long wails. As he entered the home, he found his wife Giuseppa giving birth to their first child. On October 27, 1885, Giuseppa gave birth to a son; they named him Giuseppe.

Augustino was euphoric. He kissed his wife, told her he loved her, made sure she was warm and well, and ran outdoors to tell all of his neighbors and friends of his newborn son.

Later that day he held his newborn son and told his baby, "You will have all the things in life you will ever need. I will make sure of that." Baby Giuseppe was in a sound sleep.

This pledge turned out to be one that Augustino would not be able to fulfill as easily as he'd thought he would. Although Augustino worked long hours every day on his farm to raise his pigs, chickens, and a few crops, he could not earn a profit worthy of his labor. Augustino made only meager earnings, barely enough money to support his family, to give them shelter, food, and clothing.

Augustino was not the only struggling farmer in Fornelli. These were lean times for many Italians. Outdated farming methods and the lack of soil fertilizers caused crops to yield poorly and improperly. Italians believed putting manure or decayed vegetation on the soil would contaminate the vegetables, so their lands were unfertilized. Pastures were of poor quality, livestock herds scarce and small. The government was of no help in educating its farmers, and there was much political unrest.

As a young boy, Giuseppe would help his father around the farm by feeding the animals, getting water for them, and cleaning up after them. Giuseppe loved the farm and the chores that helped his family. Giuseppe did not know his family was poor. His parents loved him, he had friends to play with, and he had the animals on the farm that he could take care of and play with as well. While Giuseppe loved his simple life, Augustino wanted more for his son. He was tired of struggling. He wanted to provide his family with comforts only higher wages could afford. Although Giuseppa never complained to her beloved Augustino, she too was tired of being poor. She prayed every night for life to improve for her family, but her prayers went unanswered.

Early one morning in the winter of 1894, Augustino went outside to fetch firewood for the cast iron cook stove in his kitchen. This stove was not only for cooking but also for warming the tiny Rossi home. There was an eerie silence in the air. No one was around, and none of Augustino's animals were stirring. Without much thought to the quiet, Augustino took the firewood into the house and placed it by the cook stove. He loaded a few small pieces of wood into the stove and turned the dampers closed so the wood would not burn too quickly.

Giuseppa and Giuseppe were asleep, and Augustino left the house to go to the farm. With one large barn, a fenced corral, and a few smaller sheds, the farm was large enough to contain the modest number of chickens and pigs that Augustino bred and raised for sale to the local markets.

As Augustino reached the corral area, he became acutely aware of that uncomfortable quietness once again. He opened the door to the barn that housed the chickens and got a sick feeling in his stomach. It was quiet—too quiet. Instead of the usual clacking and clattering of chickens, it was dead quiet. Sure enough, walking around the barn, Augustino found his chickens dead and dying. He could not believe his eyes. Out of the five hundred chickens he was fostering for the market, only one hundred or so were still alive, and those remaining looked sickly enough to warrant being destroyed. Augustino immediately went to the small open shed outside the barn to check on his five pigs. The pigs appeared to be cold but otherwise healthy. The one goat on the farm was fine as well.

Augustino was stunned. He could not understand what had happened to his chickens. He ran to his neighbors' farms to see if they'd had a similar fate. They had not. The other farmers could not believe what Augustino told them and began gathering outside his barn. One of the other farmer's wives ran to the Rossi house and roused Giuseppa from sleep to inform her. Without a sound and within seconds she dressed in warm clothing and headed to the farm with Giuseppe. Walking as quickly as she could pull Giuseppe along, she found Augustino outside the chicken barn sobbing. He would not let her or Giuseppe go inside the barn. Not only did he not want them to see the devastation of the dead animals, but he also he was afraid for their safety. Augustino sent his wife and son back home. On no past occasion had Giuseppa seen Augustino so upset. Before she left the barnyard, Giuseppa hugged her husband and told him that they would survive this.

With the help of other farmers, Augustino cleaned up the dead chickens and destroyed the remaining live ones. They dug a large, shallow trench and buried the chickens near the barn. As they cleared the dead chickens, Augustino and the other farmers looked for evidence as to what may have happened. When they got to the chicken feed storage bins, they found that mice had eaten through the floorboards and had nested deep within the grain piles. There were mice droppings throughout the piles of chicken feed. The farmers assumed that the chickens had eaten the mouse droppings, become sick, and then died. Augustino was upset and fiercely angry; doubt and sadness overcame him. Why did this have to happen to him? Why now?

Augustino was exhausted. Still, he continued until all of the chicken feed had been cleaned out of his barn. He then inspected the bins where he kept the pig feed but found no damage and no holes. The goat's food storage was intact as well. Augustino closed the door to the empty barn. He thanked the farmers who had helped him all day and then walked home. Augustino arrived at his home just after the sun had set, emotionally defeated, tired, and hungry. Giuseppa had expected such an arrival and prepared him a hearty meal in advance. Giuseppa did not speak to her husband, not even to ask questions. She knew how upset he must be and waited for him to talk when he wanted to.

After Augustino ate his pasta fagioli soup, he looked around the small kitchen and saw that there was food all around and packages of dried fruits and nuts. As he prepared to place the food in the icebox, he asked, "What is all this food, Giuseppa? Where did it come from?"

Giuseppa explained that some of the local farmers' wives had gotten together after they heard the news and put together baskets for the Rossi's. Augustino was overwhelmed, and his eyes filled with tears.

"I will thank them in the morning," he said to his wife. Giuseppa had never seen her husband this upset, and she began to cry.

The next morning Augustino got up from a restless night's sleep, washed and dressed, and headed out the door. He grabbed some of the donated dried fruit and nuts as he left. It was a new day, he thought. He could and would cope with what had happened and move on—his family would too.

As he arrived at the barn, he found the farmers who'd helped him the day before leaning on the corral fence. Augustino greeted them and thanked them for their immense generosity. Surprised by their presence so early in the morning, Augustino asked why they were there. One of the men told Augustino that they were there to inspect the pigs and goat in the daylight to see if they too were sick. They were concerned that Rossi's other animals would need to be put down as well. Fearing their own animals could become sick; they weren't there to support Augustino but to secure their own livelihoods. Augustino instantly became angry, but he restrained himself. These men were his friends, and they really meant no personal harm. The five pigs and goat were the only livestock that Augustino had to bring to market, though—his family's only livelihood.

The men inspected the pigs and goat and decided that while the pigs and goat did not appear to be sick, they would keep checking for signs of sickness regularly throughout the next few days. Augustino agreed with the men, and they left the farm. Augustino feared the farmers might return and kill his livestock. He waited until it got dark outside and then took his pigs and goat to his home. Once there he placed the pigs in the dirt crawl space under the tiny house and tied up the goat in the rear of the house. Giuseppa knew something strange was going on.

Early the next day, Augustino took his pigs and goat to the market. They arrived just as the sun came up. Salvatore the livestock buyer, who recognized Augustino, approached him.

"Good morning, Mr. Rossi. How can I help you this morning?"

Augustino acknowledged his acquaintance. "Good morning, Salvatore. I would like to sell my pigs and goat, sir. Can you purchase them?"

Salvatore inspected the livestock; because he knew Augustino, a deal was made easily. Augustino felt good about selling off his livestock. He wished he could have sold them for more money, but he had still made a good deal. At least he now had some funds to carry his family through a few winter months.

Giuseppa (Josephine) Rossi

4 INVITATION TO AMERICA

A few weeks had passed when Giuseppa told Augustino of a letter she had written to relatives in America. Augustino was not even aware of any relatives in America. "Why did you write to them?" he asked.

"My mother's sister married a man named Mr. Lancellotta. They live in America, and they have children. My mother just told me I have cousins in America too," she explained. "And so she gave me their address just three weeks ago."

"Why did you write to them?" Augustino asked again.

"Well, because I have heard other people talk about America. Some of our own neighbors are thinking of moving there. So I wrote to my relatives to ask them about it, and I told them what happened to your chickens and our farm. My aunt has written a letter back to me—can I read it to you?"

Augustino was bewildered. He had not expected this conversation. Giuseppa never displayed any sign of discontent with their modest life. He did not know whether to be upset, happy, or sad. He decided to be calm and listen to his wife. After all, he had only a small amount of money to live on—certainly not enough to invest in more livestock. Augustino agreed to listen; Giuseppa began to read the letter.

December 14, 1894

Dearest Giuseppa,

America is a land of opportunity. Here in Rhode Island there is plenty of work. You can work in the city or on a farm if you like. You can work in a large factory or a small store. You can buy a home or a piece of land to build on. You can fish the ocean or work the land. You can raise a family here and prosper. We have good neighbors and friends who are honest and hardworking. The children attend a school that is close by. They love to play in the schoolyard. The church near our home is beautiful. It is new and it sits high on a hill. Winter can be difficult here, but spring, summer, and fall are great. If you decide to move here, your uncle and I will do everything in our power to help you get started. The children would love to meet their cousin Giuseppe. Give our love to Augustino and Giuseppe.

Love,

Maria Lancellotta

Augustino could hear and feel the excitement coming from his wife's voice. Giuseppa waited for a response from her husband. Deep down inside, Augustino felt some excitement too, but he did not let on to Giuseppa.

"What do you think? Should we go to America?" she asked.

"Let me think about this," he said. "Let's ask Giuseppe what he thinks of the idea." Giuseppe, who was playing outside, came in as he heard his name mentioned. "What do you know of America?" Augustino asked his son.

"Some of my friends and their families have gone to America," he replied. "Is it far, Papa? Can we go too? Maybe I can see my friends there, and we can play."

"America is a far place to go to," Augustino explained to his son. "If we go there, we must sell our home and our farm. We will never see this place and our home ever again."

Giuseppe thought for a moment and asked, "Can we have a farm in America? Can I see my friends there?" Like any young boy, his concerns centered mostly on his friends.

"It may be possible to own a farm there, Giuseppe, but I don't know if we will see your friends. They may have moved to a different place. You might have to make new friends, but there are also many more opportunities for your future there."

"Hmmm…yes, I would like to go to America," Giuseppe told his father. Augustino looked towards Giuseppa and saw her smile.

"Give me a few days to think about this," he told her. "I need to think about it," he repeated.

Augustino put on his winter coat. As he grabbed the door handle to the front door, he told his wife, "I'm going to the barn. I need to think." As he turned the door handle to leave, he spun around, looked at his wife and son, and said, "I love you both."

Augustino stepped outside, closed the door, and stopped in his tracks. He felt the sun shining on his face. It was a beautiful day. As he looked around, he saw that the flowers that he'd planted in the fall were beginning to bloom, and their fragrance lightly scented the air. The neighbors were outside their homes cleaning, mending wooden fences, and making repairs from winter storm damage. Augustino smiled. He felt good; he felt alive and motivated. He continued on the cobblestone path, looking to the rolling hills surrounding the idyllic town. "Good morning," he said as he passed his neighbors.

"Buongiorno, Augustino," they responded.

Augustino arrived at the empty barn and opened its two large front doors. It was warm outside now. Augustino removed his coat, grabbed a free wooden stool, and sat down by the door opening. He sat there, picking his teeth with a piece of straw, for almost two hours when suddenly a stranger approached.

"Buongiorno," Augustino said to the well-dressed man as he approached.

The man wearing a silk shirt, pressed trousers, and shiny black shoes walked up to Augustino and extended his hand. They shook hands—both with a firm grip. "Good morning to you, sir. Are you the owner of this property?" he asked.

Augustino said, "Yes, I am the owner."

"My name is Dominic," he explained. "I represent some businessmen from Napoli who are looking to purchase property in this area to expand their investment holdings. Might you be interested in selling your property, sir?"

Augustino, in a state of disbelief, looked up toward the heavens and then back into the eyes of the man in front of him. Augustino knew he had to make a split-second decision and that what he was about to say could change the lives of himself and his family forever. *Can this really be happening? Is it meant to be?*

"Yes!" Augustino said to the man. "I have been considering the sale of my farm and home. However, both must be sold in order for me to purchase another property."

Dominic smiled at Augustino. "May I inspect your farm today and come back tomorrow to view your home?" he asked. "Perhaps we can come to terms afterwards," he said.

"Si, si. Of course," Augustino replied.

The two men then wandered around the farm and inspected the buildings, equipment, crops, and remaining animals, and then parted for the day. Augustino rushed home. He could not wait to tell his wife what had happened. Giuseppa's eyes filled with tears as Augustino explained to her the day's unexpected events.

Giuseppa looked toward a small statue of the Virgin Mary with a candle burning and then back toward Augustino. "I've been praying," she said.

That afternoon and into the late evening, Augustino and Giuseppa worked around their home, cleaning, straightening, and preparing for their visitor. Rising early the next morning, and without any words, Giuseppa and Augustino finished their chores.

By midmorning, everything was in its proper place, even Giuseppe's room. The house looked terrific, inside and out. Giuseppa baked *ciambella* (sugar-coated fried pastry) and brewed a fresh pot of coffee. As she was taking the ciambella from the cast iron oven, Dominic arrived; he knocked lightly on the door. Giuseppe heard the knock and hopped to the door, arriving there at the same time as his mother. They glanced at each other and opened the door. Giuseppa admired how handsome and well dressed Dominic was. "This is my son, Giuseppe," she said. "I am Giuseppa."

Dominic introduced himself. He too admired how attractive Giuseppa was. Giuseppa had creamy-looking skin, dark eyes, and long, dark hair. Although she wearing an apron, Dominic could see that she had a slender figure.

Augustino approached the two from the back house. "Buongiorno and welcome to our home," he greeted Dominic. As Dominic entered the home, he was overwhelmed by the sweet scents and rich espresso. Giuseppa steered Dominic to the small kitchen area.

"Please have ciambella and café with us," she said.

"I would like that very much," he responded.

Dominic, Augustino, and Giuseppa sat and made conversation as if they were old friends. For nearly an hour, they talked about different subjects and, surprisingly, not a word about the property. Dominic, who was still admiring Giuseppa's beauty, was calm and professional.

"There is no need for me to see the rest of the property," he said.

Augustino and Giuseppa looked at each other, afraid that there was some problem. Before they could speak, Dominic continued.

"You have a very nice home and farm. It is easy for me to see that you have maintained your property. I am prepared to make you an offer for your property, and you are under no pressure to sell if you decide not to accept my offer."

Dominic gave Augustino and Giuseppa an amount that he was willing to pay for the Rossi property.

"I have learned what other similar properties in your neighborhood have sold for, and I feel this is a fair offering. Please take some time to consider my offer. I will return in a few days for your answer."

As he got up from his chair to leave, Dominic shook hands with Augustino. "Will you be moving to America as many of your neighbors have?" he asked.

Augustino, who was incapable of telling a lie, said, "It is most likely that we will."

Dominic turned to Giuseppa and looked her squarely in the eye as he took her hand. "Thank you for your generosity and for allowing me into your home," he said. He gave her a gentleman's kiss on each cheek and then left the Rossi house.

My great-grandparents were unaware that many of their neighbors were relocating to the United States. Millions of immigrants would make the journey from many points in Europe. Most were accepted in the United States; others were deported and sent back to their homelands. All were seeking the streets paved with gold. The majority would lead good lives as they worked hard and prospered. The Rossi family made the long journey and survived the detailed immigration checkpoints of Ellis Island. With the aid of my great-grandmother's relatives, they would travel to the smallest state in the Union, but one of the fastest growing, Rhode Island. They would settle into a small hamlet called Natick in May 1895. My grandfather, Giuseppe, was ten years old.

5 A NEW BEGINNING

By ten years of age, Giuseppe had experienced an ocean voyage aboard a large passenger ship and the sights and sounds that were New York City: large towering buildings of concrete, paved roads, sidewalks, and street lamps. The sights of railroad locomotives and railcars, crowded streets, storefronts, and shipping ports thrilled him. Men, women, and children dressed in clothing that he was not accustomed to seeing and spoke languages foreign to him. Fire trucks and police sirens were wailing through the streets. As Giuseppe and his family passed through to Providence, he noticed the bustling factories and knew he would work in one someday as an adult. By the year of 1896, when Giuseppe was eleven, there were at least 140 factories within a thirty-mile radius of Providence, mostly textile mills.

Augustino, Guiseppa, and Guiseppe moved into a small single room at the Lancellotta house in Natick, Rhode Island. Natick was a town of large textile mills built of stone or brick and small houses—many of which were owned by the textile mills and rented to the workers of those mills. There were several mansions owned by wealthy textile mill owners and some large farm properties. Much of the industry in Natick was built along the Pawtuxet River. Large dams were instrumental in converting waterpower and providing mechanical power to the mills. The Willimantic Branch of the New York, New Haven and Hartford Railroad was busy pulling railcar loads of textiles and other goods. Most factories had railroad tracks beside their property; some had private loading docks and direct access to the rail system. Giuseppe observed such details; he was amazed by the technicality and planning of it all.

The Rossis' temporary new home at the Lancellottas' was sufficient since they had few material possessions and the room was rent-free. Only a short period lapsed before Augustino found suitable work. A wealthy landowner with livestock and a large parcel of land employed him. He would often work seven days a week, sunup to sundown. He enjoyed his work. He felt wanted and appreciated. The landowner provided all necessary tools

16

and equipment. Life was good, and adapting to new surroundings was easy for Augustino.

Likewise, Guiseppa adapted well to her new home. With relatives nearby, textile mills and stores in the area, and a steady income from Augustino, Giuseppa enjoyed a new outlook on life.

Giuseppe too embraced his new life. He was not afraid or intimidated by any of the new sights, sounds, or bustling lifestyles in America. Instead, he was excited and wanted to see more. Giuseppe played with his cousins in their backyard and was eager for them to take him to see new things. Language was a small barrier, but it turned out to be half the fun. The cousins tried to figure out what each other was saying through hand signals and pictures drawn in the sand. There was a rope swing hanging from a high branch of a tall tree and a seesaw that looked like it would break the next time one of them sat on it. There was also a horseshoe-throwing court in the backyard, but only the adults were allowed to use it.

Giuseppe's cousins and their friends introduced him to fishing in the Pawtuxet and placing pennies on the nearby railroad tracks. When they heard the train coming, they would hide beside the tracks after placing a coin on the rail. The heavy locomotive and railcars passed over the coins and flattened them. Sometimes the coin would disappear completely. Other times the coins would be tossed far down the tracks, and the boys would have to search for the ejected coins. Giuseppe had never experienced anything like it.

Giuseppe attended school with his cousins. They could already read and write in English, and school was not the least bit difficult for them. For Giuseppe, it was not so easy; although he lived in a predominately Italian neighborhood, not all of the teachers could translate for him nor did they make much effort to. At school, there were many French-Canadian children and many of the teachers spoke French. This was frustrating for Giuseppe. He wanted to learn to read and write English, to fit in and be part of the American landscape, and to be accepted by his peers. Over time Giuseppe would learn to speak, read, and write English, however imperfectly.

At about twelve years old, Giuseppe thought little of his schooling and began to work part time at any factory that accepted him. He was employed to sweep the oily wooden floors, pick up trash on the mill property, lubricate the textile looms, and perform other menial tasks. In those days, a twelve-year-old boy could earn one dollar a week.

Giuseppe loved being in the factory with the noisy chattering of its machinery. There were spinning shafts of steel with steel wheels of various diameters attached to the ends located throughout the factory. On these steel wheels were long leather belts or straps that would come down from the ceiling and connect to steel drive wheels on all the machinery. For many of the older factories, all of this drive train was perpetuated by a large wood and steel paddle wheel, which was being rotated by the waterfall in the river beside the factory. Some of the newer factories had large steam engines, which had boilers fired with coal or wood.

Giuseppe, intrigued by all of this mechanical activity, was quickly accepted by the mill mechanics, also known as the "millwrights." They taught him to disassemble the textile looms and other machinery to affect repairs. Before long, Giuseppe was proficient at making repairs and keeping the machinery operating and lubricated, and he became indispensable to the factory.

Having a formal education became less and less a priority in Giuseppe's life compared to earning a good week's pay. By the time he was in his mid- to late teens, he was self-sufficient. Not only could he provide for himself, but he also contributed to his parents' welfare by paying for his own room and board. Giuseppe would take any extra money he had at the end of the week and put it aside in a savings stash that only he knew about. As time passed, he was able to squirrel away a respectable sum of cash.

In 1906, at age twenty-one, Giuseppe was fully independent and mature. Although he loved his work, he realized that he had spent most of his teen years inside of textile factories. In his conversations with co-workers, mostly older Italian immigrants, Giuseppe would hear stories of his native country of Italy and his mountaintop hometown of Fornelli. He began to daydream of visiting his homeland someday.

Textile machinery

6 RESEARCH BEGINS, 1992

I started researching my grandfather's story back in 1992 when I purchased my first computer. At that time, computers and the Internet were a time-consuming venture. You needed direction, unlike today. Search engines on the net are much more advanced now, and information is abundant—the world is literally at your fingertips.

For years I've collected information and books about World Wars I and II. I have printed reams of paper on articles about weaponry, soldiers, and national leaders. On Saturday mornings, my wife and I would browse antique shops. She would look for home décor items while I sought out old books from the 1940s with articles about Hitler and his secret weapons: the Buzz Bombs, V1 and V2 rockets.

The flying robot plane that my grandfather had designed was essentially the bomb that never blew. In an era well after my grandfather's passing, Adolph Hitler's rocket scientist, Wernher Von Braun, released the revolutionary Buzz Bomb, aka the Vengeance or Doodle Bug bomb. The Von Braun V1 weapon used in World War II made its debut in June of 1944—as it was unleashed on London. I noticed that the weapon was similar to my grandfather's invention in appearance and it operated in nearly the same manner.

Finding information about Von Braun and other scientists was motivating. I continued to do my book searches, online scans, and antique store scavenging to try to find what little information I could about aerial bombs and remote controlled devices.

A few years later, in July 1997, my father passed away. I realized that I had lost my best friend and that I knew little to nothing of his parents. I remember my grandmother Rossi (my father's mom) from childhood, but I have only a few memories spending time with her. My grandmother was an excellent cook. She mixed up a great pot of Italian wedding soup when we visited her, and she spoke with a thick Italian accent. She would give us kids big wet kisses on the cheek.

When I was only thirteen years old, my grandmother passed away. In her second-floor bedroom, at the foot of her bed, was her old black steamer trunk that she had used to come to the United States from Italy with Giuseppe. In it she kept warm thick blankets and personal items. Neither my father nor his six brothers ever divulged any information about their father when I asked about him and his invention. Instead they said that they did not remember because they were too young. They would feed me a tidbit of information and then change the subject. They could not understand my curiosity.

"Our father tried to become successful with his invention and missed the mark," they would say. "He is long gone, along with the model [prototype]." I sensed that there was a story that needed telling, and it was not going to come from them. I'd have to find out the truth myself. There was a well-kept family secret there.

One day I watched a program on television about the evolution of the flying weaponry of WWII, which got me even more serious about researching my grandfather's device.

In the fall of 2000, I decided to increase my research efforts by trying to find my grandfather's actual patent in the records provided by the National Archives and Records Administration on the web. I had the patent number and a description of the device but could not locate specific records on the net. I entered keyword descriptions like "aerial torpedo," "Buzz Bomb," and "robot plane." These searches yielded meager and inconclusive results.

The National Archives website had a link where you could obtain further information on patents and inventors, so I inquired with what little information I could provide in the spaces allowed. Weeks went by, and I received no response. It felt like a long shot, and I was beginning to think it was a lost cause.

Then on December 9, 2000, I received a letter from the National Archives and Records Administration. I rushed to open it and was amazed to find it contained an application to order a copy of my grandfather's invention patent. Part of the form had been filled out with internal information such as the patent file's location, the stock number, and the patent file number. The letter also contained a note:

"A copy of your (email) request has been forwarded to our Military Records staff. You will be hearing from them shortly concerning any correspondence with your grandfather from the War and Navy Departments."

I quickly filled out the form and sent it back with a letter:

December 10, 2000

To Whom It May Concern:

Thank you for your personal attention to my request for records and documents concerning my grandfather, Giuseppe Rossi. I am sending a copy of a newspaper article regarding his invention. I hope that it may help locate documentation pertaining to his device. Although there are no dates mentioned, this information may be beneficial to you. I am enclosing the $12.00 processing and documentation fee for the patent copy. I am excited to get a new copy of his patent, and am hopeful that other documentation can be located as well

Sincerely,

Richard Rossi

In addition to this letter and a copy of the newspaper article, I included a copy of my California driver's license. I had nothing to hide and everything to gain. I placed these items neatly in a large envelope addressed to the National Archives located in College Park, Maryland, on Adelphia Road.

I assumed that in two or three weeks I would receive the copied patent. By December 18, 2000, my twelve-dollar check had been cashed and cleared. Yet—no patent. I figured maybe the holidays were slowing things down.

By January 22, more than a month on, I still had not received the patent copy. I decided to fill out another request form, wrote another twelve-dollar check, and placed a note in the envelope stating that this was a second request for this information and that my first check had been cashed but I had not received my copied patent. I hoped persistence would achieve results.

Shortly after I sent the second request, I received a letter from 700 Pennsylvania Avenue, Washington, DC, the National Archives and Records Administration. It was a response to a different inquiry I had made regarding my grandfather's visit to Washington back in the nineteen hundreds. It was concise:

Dear Sir,

We examined indexes to the Bureau of Ordnance general correspondence, Office of the Secretary of the Navy correspondence, the Navy's "invention file," and records of the Naval Consulting Board, a committee that evaluated inventions for the Navy Department. We did not locate a reference to Giuseppe Rossi or his invention of an aerial torpedo.

National Archives and Records Administration

I thought this response was unusual. My newspaper article clearly stated that "the War and Navy Departments said they had no use" for the weapon, which led me to believe that they did, in fact, have knowledge of the device and my grandfather's correspondence with the War and Navy Departments.

The article I had also stated that my grandfather wrote to the War Department in regards to another invention in 1916 and was later approached at his workplace by an army ordnance officer sent by the War Department who monitored my grandfather's progress on the aerial torpedo. There had to be a record. It must have been overlooked or misfiled—but hopefully not discarded. I was sure the army had worked with my grandfather and his device.

Early in February 2001, I still had not received anything from Washington. I thought perhaps that someone would contact me to verify my relationship with Giuseppe Rossi. Or, worse, tell me that his files could not be located.

On my birthday—February 17—in 2001, a large envelope arrived in the mailbox. The return address on the envelope was Adelphia Road, College Park, Maryland; inside the envelope was a copy of my grandfather's patent. The envelope contained eleven letter-size documents and sixteen legal-size documents. All were new, crisp, black-and-white photocopies of the documentation of my grandfather's invention. Although a few of the pages indicated some wear, the majority of the documents were as fresh as the day they were originally printed some eighty years before.

One page that listed the contents of the documentation package was clearly tattered along the edges from exposure to the ambient air. In the upper left-hand corner of the page, I noticed that the copier had left a triangular black spot, as if a cover page had been folded back from the content list and then placed into the photocopier. I needed to find out if a page had been omitted.

I was holding in my hands a small piece of United States history initiated by my grandfather, an immigrant with a dream. It was the first time I had seen my grandfather's signature. I stopped and stared at it for a long period, analyzing its every stroke. It was very similar to my dad's signature, another Rossi with limited education but immense capability. Vivid drawings and descriptions of the device, as well as signatures and dates from those who were instrumental in documenting this invention, were as clear as they must have been the day they were produced. I had some new avenues to research.

Giuseppe Rossi,
(Inventor's Signature.)

7 VISIT TO ITALY

In spring 1906, Giuseppe decided to pay a visit to Italy. At twenty-one years old, with what seemed like a lifetime of working years behind him, he decided he needed an adventure. The ship ride to Italy took longer than he had remembered as a boy traveling to the United States. Once on Italian soil, he made his way by train from the city of Naples to a station in Campobasso, a distance from Fornelli. It was late in the evening when he finally arrived in Fornelli; it was cold and about to rain. As he walked toward the village entrance, Giuseppe remembered the village stonewall entrance. The wall was now covered with green moss, but he recognized it as part of his childhood home.

As he walked down the narrow, tree-lined cobblestone road he came upon the house of his childhood. It was dark outside now, but there was enough light for him to see, and he did not want to disturb the home's current occupants. Giuseppe made his way to what had once been his father's barn. He found the double doors unlocked, and he went inside to total darkness and quiet. It had begun to rain, and he was cold. He fumbled in the dark on the planked floor and decided to lie down. Excited, but extremely weary, he fell asleep right there and didn't stir until midmorning.

Through holes in the roof and walls, rays of sunlight roused him from sleep. He heard voices speaking his native tongue, Italian. He ached from sleeping on the hard floor and urgently needed to relieve himself. He remembered seeing an outhouse nearby the night before and decided he had better get there quickly. As he left the barn, he encountered and startled two men of about his age.

The first young man, tall and skinny with light brown hair, was a bit frightened. "Who are you?" he mumbled.

The second young man, short and stout with black hair, was more forward. "And what are you doing in this old barn?"

Giuseppe, who was undeterred by the two men, put his hands on each of their shoulders, glanced at each of them, and said, "I am Giuseppe Rossi. I once lived here," and pushed them to one side.

The two men stood there, mouths agape, as Giuseppe headed for the outhouse. When he opened the door to leave, Giuseppe found the two men still standing outside the outhouse. Giuseppe was cautious and became defensive. "Who are you two? What do you want?" he blurted in Italian.

"If you are Giuseppe Rossi, then what are your parents' names?" one man asked.

"Yeah and where are they now?" asked the other.

"I am the son of Augustino and Giuseppa. They are living in America now," Giuseppe answered.

The two men looked at each other, paused, and began to laugh and scream, "It's Giuseppe Rossi. It's Giuseppe Rossi." They grabbed Giuseppe by his coat and spun him in circles, chanting, "It's Giuseppe Rossi! It is really Giuseppe Rossi!"

Giuseppe, who was still tired and very hungry, defensively grabbed each man by his arm and flung him to the ground. The men, now covered in mud from the rain the night before, were stunned. "And what sack of nuts did you two fall from?" Giuseppe said, shaking off his dizziness.

With a big grin on his face, one man yelled, "I am Alberic."

The other man yelled, "And I am Biagio. Do you not remember us? We are the Di Domenici brothers!"

Brothers? These two couldn't look more different. Giuseppe stepped back and leaned against the fence post with *his* mouth now hanging open and his eyes rolling and said, "Si, I remember now."

The three men shook hands and laughed. They had been best of friends as children and had not seen each other for eleven years. "Let us take you to the café near here for food and drink," Alberic said.

"Yes, we want to hear all about America," said Biagio.

As the trio headed for the pub, Giuseppe said, "I need to see my old home first and meet the people that live there."

"You can see your old home, Giuseppe, but no one lives there. The place is empty."

"Families come and go from this village. There is not much work here to earn your keep. Times haven't changed much since your family emigrated."

When they got to the old house, Giuseppe went inside. He remembered it well—though the house was now empty and in disrepair. The walls were dirty and had holes, and it seemed much smaller than he remembered. He went to the kitchen. He remembered his mother making ciambella, the sweet smell of cinnamon and sugar. He remembered how his father would stack wood for the stove.

His visit was brief but filled with memories. The men then left the house and went to the pub where they spent hours laughing, eating, and remembering their childhood days.

Giuseppe was invited to the home of Signor and Signora Di Domenici, which was nearby. For the next two days, the three friends visited people and places Giuseppe wanted to see. Soon enough, Giuseppe felt uncomfortable imposing on his friends' parents. He offered them money to repay their kindness, but they refused his offer.

Giuseppe asked Alberic and Biagio to take him to a General Store, *un negozio digeneri alimentari.* There, Giuseppe loaded Biagio and Alberic's arms with meat, bread, preserves, and flour. They returned to the Di Domenici home, and Giuseppe presented the goods to his friends' parents. They were grateful and showered Giuseppe with praise and thanks. Giuseppe announced that he had enjoyed his time visiting Fornelli, but that he must return to Rhode Island.

Alberic and Biagio, who were sitting down, jumped up simultaneously, grabbed Giuseppe by the arms, and in unison said, "No, you can't leave us!"

"We are going to visit and maybe work for our uncle in Campobasso," they told him. "We would like you to come with us. If you don't want to stay after you see the place, we will understand. The train station is close by, and you can leave from there."

Giuseppe agreed to the offer (because of its proximity to the train station), and the three men departed the next morning.

They traveled east for two hours on the train to reach Campobasso. They were comforted by Giuseppe's presence since he was a bona fide world traveler already. He was smart and would protect them, they reasoned. When they arrived, they were amazed to see such a modern city. There were elaborate buildings, paved streets, gas lamp lighting, trolley cars, and automobiles. People were much more stylish than in Fornelli, wearing the latest fashions. It reminded Giuseppe of Providence, Rhode Island. In a sense, he felt at home.

Signor Giovanni and Signora Maria Di Domenici greeted the three at their doorstep and welcomed them.

Biagio turned to Giuseppe and said, "Hey have you met our cousin Vin—"

Alberic pushed his brother, smiled, and interjected, "Ah, you will meet our cousin soon enough."

"Your cousin is at work right now but will be home soon," said Mrs. Di Domenici smiling (almost laughing) at her nephews. "Lunch is ready if anyone is hungry."

The young men bolted toward the kitchen.

They talked of Mr. Di Domenici's plumbing and construction business. "I could use the help of three strong young men at my business, if you are interested," he said. "It's hard, back-breaking work, and I have plenty of it," he added.

Alberic and Biagio shied away from their uncle. Giuseppe was unafraid of hard work but said that he did not expect to be in town for long. "I have a job back in—"

From the front door came a knock. Mrs. Di Domenici went to see who was at the door. She turned the handle and pulled, but the door was locked; she unlocked the door and opened it.

"Mama, who locked the door?" the young woman asked as she entered the house. The young woman put down some packages she was carrying and removed her heavy coat. The three young men heard the young woman's voice and proceeded toward its source in the living room. "Introduce your cousin to Giuseppe," said Mrs. Di Domenici to her nephews.

Biagio spoke up, "Giuseppe Rossi, please meet our cousin Vin—"

"Vincenza," Alberic interrupted, and the two men laughed heartily.

Standing in front of Giuseppe was a beautiful young woman with a round face, sparkling dark eyes, and long brown hair. She made eye contact with Giuseppe and smiled. He reached out, took her hand, and smiled back. "It is a pleasure to meet you, Vincenza," he said. In the same breath, he turned to her father and with a fast change of heart said, "Can we start work tomorrow, Mr. Di?"

The family laughed, except for Vincenza. She was not sure what had just taken place. Mr. Di Domenici placed his hand on Giuseppe's shoulder and said, "Yes, tomorrow would be a good day for the three of you to get started." Alberic and Biagio rolled their eyes in discontent but said nothing. "That's if you can let go of my daughter's hand by then," he said. The family laughed.

Giuseppe looked back at Vincenza, smiling, and reluctantly released her hand. Vincenza, now blushing, asked, "Did you boys save me any lunch? I'm starving."

Immediately after breakfast the following morning, Mr. Di Domenici took the young men to his job site, not too far away. Giuseppe, Alberic, and Biagio rode in the back of Mr. Di Domenici's stake body truck. The three had to stand up by the cab of the truck and hold on tightly because the truck was designed to withstand the rugged terrain of a construction site. It had hard rubber tires and rode terribly. When they arrived, there was another truck with supplies and two more men awaiting them.

After introductions, Mr. Di Domenici went to the rear of the enclosed truck and handed each man a shovel and pick. He escorted them to the spot where they would spend the next few days digging long deep trenches.

"We will be installing a cast iron water main throughout this street," he said. "I need you to dig a trench two feet wide and five feet deep. When the trench is long enough, the other two men will install the pipe and put a foot of dirt on top. One of you will need to finish refilling the trench with dirt. We have soaked the trench area with water, so the digging should not be too difficult. Any questions?"

The trio looked at Mr. Di Domenici and shook their heads no. As Mr. Di walked away, the men looked down the street to see just how long it was, but they could not even see the end. When their uncle was out of sight, Alberic and Biagio began to complain to Giuseppe. "We must be crazy to be here," said Alberic.

"We're only doing this for you, Giuseppe. I hope you realize that," said Biagio.

"Stop your bellyaching, and let's get to work," Giuseppe laughingly replied. He took the first shovel of dirt and tossed it aside—the other boys followed his lead.

Mr. Di Domenici had a scheduled deadline that he was not sure he could keep. Delays in gathering materials, groundwater in the trench, and large boulders presented almost daily problems. Giuseppe, Alberic, and Biagio began working sunup to sundown every day, including weekends. Fortunately, Vincenza brought them food each day and—to his delight—spent time with Giuseppe as he ate. Soon they became good friends.

Mr. Di Domenici had an agreement with his trenching crew to house and feed them until the project was finished. He could not pay them salary until he received payment in full from his client after the work was completed. Giuseppe had pocket change remaining from the funds he'd brought from home in Rhode Island. The scheduled deadline forced him to work harder and to push Alberic and Biagio to near exhaustion.

At the site, Mr. Di Domenici taught Giuseppe the art and use of explosives. Common explosives like dynamite sticks were necessary to cut through the huge rocks encountered while trenching. Mr. Di would have apprenticed Alberic or Biagio, but he was reluctant due to their lack of attentiveness and responsibility. Explosives required thoughtfulness and caution—neither Alberic nor Biagio's strong suit.

Meanwhile, Giuseppe mostly looked forward to Vincenza's lunch delivery visits each day. As much as he appreciated and enjoyed Mr. Di's lessons, he was disappointed and sullen whenever Vincenza did not show—which was on several occasions.

The men continued to work so hard for Mr. Di that they ended up completing the pipeline project in twenty-eight days—four days fewer than projected. Mr. Di Domenici was ecstatic and so thankful that he took his crew to a local pub to celebrate. The men ate, drank, and laughed until early the next morning.

Feeling groggy and a bit hungover, Giuseppe finally awoke around noon to the rich smell of espresso and fresh baked sweet rolls. He knew it had to be Vincenza in the kitchen. He quickly splashed some water on his face, brushed back his hair, and made his way to the kitchen.

From their lunchtime chats, Vincenza knew that Giuseppe loved fresh coffee and sweet rolls in the morning. She expected him to be the first to enter the kitchen.

They greeted each other happily with their eyes before speaking. A smile spread wide on each of their faces as they expressed a joyful "Buongiorno."

Giuseppe felt a sensation come over him unlike any he'd felt before. His head was spinning, his mouth was dry, and his stomach was fluttering. He wondered if maybe he'd gotten up too quickly. Perhaps he was ill from excessive alcohol the night before. Or on the other hand, was he just hungry? Maybe it was a lack of food making him feel so out of sorts.

He and Vincenza spoke softly in the kitchen so as not to wake the others in the house. He realized that he was so excited to see *her* that it was literally making him dizzy. In her apron, with oven mitts on her hands, her long brown hair tied into a ponytail, her bright smile, and beautiful eyes, Giuseppe was about ready to fall over. He knew then—he was in love.

Vincenza came closer to pour a cup of coffee for Giuseppe. Before she could, Giuseppe took her into his arms and kissed her. Filled with a sense of excitement, he whispered to her, "I love you."

"I love you too," she replied glowingly, looking more radiant to Giuseppe than ever.

The next day Mr. Di Domenici paid each of the men the wages he'd promised. He took Giuseppe aside and told him, "I have given you a bit extra for your exceptional hard work, your quick learning of explosives, and your 'take charge' attitude. It would have been much more difficult for me to complete this job and motivate the other men had you not been so helpful. I would like to teach you more of this business if you are willing to learn from me. I love my nephews dearly, but they are not leaders—they are followers. If you would like to stay and work for me, I could certainly use your help."

Giuseppe was deeply grateful for Mr. Di's appreciation. "Yes, sir, Mr. Di. I would very much like to learn from you, but I will need to get my own place to live. I cannot continue to impose on your hospitality."

"If that's all it will take to keep you here, then consider it taken care of. I have friends who own many properties. I am sure they can help us find you a place of your own," Mr. Di replied.

A few days later, Giuseppe was sent to a new, larger water distribution system installation project. Signor Di Domenici hired additional men and then appointed Giuseppe as construction foreman. Alberic and Biagio were excited for Giuseppe. After all, they did not wish for any responsibility, and they would still have fun working with Giuseppe. This way, the brothers could still hassle Giuseppe and get a rise out of him for the sake of a good laugh afterward. Giuseppe was enjoying his new job, his new life, and he soon had his own two-room, furnished apartment.

Mr. Di wasted no time teaching Giuseppe the ins and outs of being the foreman for the new job. He taught him all he could about pipefitting and water distribution system installation. Giuseppe learned quickly; he was a hands-on learner and absorbed everything. It was hard work, yet Giuseppe enjoyed it. Mr. Di Domenici appreciated Giuseppe's dedication and compensated him well after completing that project and all projects that followed. Giuseppe had few expenses and was able to save up much of the money he earned. He knew already that this would help guarantee him a good life, and enable him to provide for a family in the future.

In early 1907, after a brief courtship, Giuseppe asked Mr. Di Domenici for his daughter's hand in marriage. Mr. Di joyfully approved of Giuseppe and welcomed him warmly into the family. The Di Domenicis congratulated Giuseppe and Vincenza and expressed their love and enthusiasm for the couple. Alberic and Biagio began celebrating well before the marriage was to take place.

On May 18, 1907, Giuseppe and Vincenza married in the Di Domenici home. Vincenza was seventeen, and Giuseppe was twenty-two. Family and friends attended the joyous occasion. Vincenza and Giuseppe were grateful to be showered with gifts for their new life together—as husband and wife.

Mr. and Mrs. Giuseppe Rossi

Soon Giuseppe was fully in charge of his father-in-law's business, over-seeing the day-to-day operation of construction projects. As new construction projects became available, Giuseppe and his crew took on projects that larger construction companies could not be bothered with. This meant that these projects were often difficult, labor-intensive, and had a low profit margin. Giuseppe became frustrated that he could not obtain the larger, more profitable contracts for Mr. Di Domenici. He lacked the capital to purchase the most modern tools and equipment to become a competitive contractor.

In April of 1908, Vincenza became pregnant with the couple's first child. On December 8, 1908, a beautiful baby girl was born. Her parents truly believed she was an angel sent from heaven—a blessing. They named her Maria Angelina Rossi.

Maria Angelina Rossi

8 A MISSING PAGE

After pouring through the records I received, and becoming more frustrated and confused, I decided to contact the National Archives and Records Administration by phone. The thought of a possible missing page from these documents was driving me crazy. After listening to several recorded messages and countless preset options, I was finally connected to a real person named Martha.

"Hello, I'm doing a follow up on records I received by mail. I feel a page may be missing from the documents. Can you help me?"

"Why do you think a page is missing?" Martha asked.

"Because the upper right hand corner of the content list has a triangular blackened spot. It looks like a page was folded back before it was copied," I replied.

"I'm afraid you are going to have to submit a new application to the archives. The case file you previously requested has most likely been placed back in storage. Once you submit another application, the file could take up to two to three weeks to be copied and sent to you," she replied.

"But I'm looking for *one* page, and I just received these records. Is it possible the file has not been sent back to storage?" I tried my best to be as patient as possible.

"Please hold, sir."

When Martha came back, she asked if I would mind if a student volunteer could help me, that perhaps she could look at the files that are on their way back to storage. Otherwise, I would have to resubmit the application and go through the process again. Needless to say, I didn't hesitate in accepting the volunteer's help.

"This is Diana speaking. How may I help you, sir?"

I repeated the whole story. "Hello, Diana. I'm Richard Rossi. I just received records from the archives, and I feel a page may be missing. Can you check to see if the file is still available for Giuseppe Rossi?"

"Let me put you on hold, and I will check for you, sir."

A moment later Diana got back on the phone and said, "I have the file in my hand. What page do you think is missing?"

My heart quickened with excitement. What might the missing page reveal?

"It's probably the cover page. I have the contents page, but it is before that. In the upper right-hand corner of *my* copy, there is a triangular black spot, as if there was a page folded back when it was copied."

"Let me check. Yes, I have it here! There is a page attached to the contents list."

"Great, that's exciting! What does it say? Can you send me a copy?"

"No, I can't copy this page. It's simply an interoffice memo."

"Can you tell me what it says at least?"

"Oh sure. It says, 'Any inquiries regarding this patent file, please notify RMII,' and a code number, 03-021646. There is nothing else—that's all it says."

I quickly jotted this down. "What does the code number mean, and what is RMII?"

"I can't answer your questions—I'm new here—but let me ask one of our senior archivists. Would you like to hold?"

"Yes, of course," I responded.

A voice of an older woman was soon on the phone, and she introduced herself as Bette; she had the interoffice memo in her hand. She told me she had been an employee for seventeen years and that she did not know who, what, or where RMII would be in reference to in the archives building.

"Well, then can you explain the code number to me?"

She thought perhaps that 03 was a code number used in the past to indicate an incident under investigation was possibly associated with this file, and the number 021646 was most likely the date the incident took place.

I paused for a moment, thinking to myself. The phone was silent until finally I said, "Thank you, Bette, for your help and your time."

"Huh, that's strange," Bette said suddenly.

"What is it, Bette?"

"I just realized that the memo is written on DOD stationery—the paper has a faint watermark insignia that I can see in the light," she said curiously.

"DOD?"

"Sorry, Department of Defense. Back in the day it was known as the War Department." She stated she didn't have any more information and thanked me for my call.

I hung up the phone intrigued and confused by everything I just heard. A multitude of questions began spinning in my head.

021646, 02/16/46, 2-16-46. Was this really a date? That date meant nothing to me—in reference to what? And what possible "03" incidents could she be referring to? Was RMII perhaps someone's initials or could it even just mean "room 2"?

The fact that the memo was on War Department stationary, and the date, if it was a date, just did not make any sense to me.

I almost wished I hadn't called and received this information.

I could not sleep for days with these questions weighing on my mind. *Damn it, what am I missing here?*

9 RETURN TO AMERICA

In 1910, after four years of living in Italy, Giuseppe decided it was time to return to America. Although he loved his mother- and father-in-law, the plumbing contracting business was failing, and the money in his savings was dwindling. Giuseppe was working day and night trying to compete with larger companies, but in the end, he could not meet the challenge. Mr. and Mrs. Di Domenici were sad but knew this was best for their daughter and her family.

In a tearful departure, Giuseppe, Vincenza, and their daughter Maria Angelina made the long voyage to America. When they arrived in Natick, Giuseppe's parents Augustino and Giuseppa were anxiously awaiting them and couldn't be more thrilled! They eagerly awaited their son's arrival, but especially that of their new daughter-in-law and granddaughter. Vincenza had written to them often from Italy, and they and Vincenza already felt a strong connection to each other.

Only days after returning, Giuseppe was once again working in a textile mill. He was surrounded every minute by textile looms and other noise-making machinery, and loving every minute. He felt proud of all he'd accomplished in Italy but was glad to finally get home.

B.B. & R. Knight Mills

One day at the mill Giuseppe overheard a conversation between two mill workers from the office. A piece of land that was owned by the mill owners was about to be foreclosed by the city due to a large amount of outstanding back taxes. He listened carefully as one worker described the location of the property. Giuseppe knew exactly where it was and could not believe the B.B. & R. Knight Corporation owned it. One worker said to the other, "We need to *dump* that land anyway!"

Then they both laughed and walked away. Giuseppe was a little confused by their discussion and decided to see the property for himself after work. Giuseppe walked up to the property and was overwhelmed by an odor that reminded him of dirty socks, rotten food, and manure. When he took a few steps closer, he discovered what the office workers were joking about. The land was a dump—literally! The village residents had been throwing their trash onto this property for years. There was a mountain of decomposing garbage, refuse, and waste—junk!

The Pawtuxet Valley River was on one side, the New Haven/Hartford Railroad on another, and East Avenue, where a new concrete bridge was being constructed, bordered the property. Giuseppe walked around the property until daylight was gone. Despite all the mess and noise, something about this place inspired him. He decided to consult his father before jumping into a crazy land—dump—purchase.

"Am I out of my mind to think that I can clean up this piece of property?" he asked his father.

"I know that piece of property," Augustino replied. "There is good land at the bottom of all that junk, and if you can buy it for a low price, it would be worth all the hard work it will take to clean it up." Augustino smiled at his son. "But, yes! You must be a little crazy...after all you are my son!" Giuseppe laughed with his dad.

That afternoon, after work, Giuseppe went to the front office at the mill to see Mr. Robert Knight, the property owner. After waiting for a short while at the reception area, Giuseppe was escorted in to see Mr. Knight. Mr. Knight was putting a thick book onto a well-organized shelf along the wall and had his back to Giuseppe.

Mr. Knight was a tall, well-dressed man with graying hair and wire-rimmed glasses. He was a wealthy, powerful, and influential man. As Mr. Knight turned and faced his visitor, Giuseppe felt secure and only slightly intimidated as he politely introduced himself.

"Mr. Knight, I am Giuseppe Rossi," he said, extending his hand for a handshake.

Mr. Knight took Giuseppe's hand and gave it a firm shake.

"I know who you are, Giuseppe. You are one of my finest millwrights." The conversation was already off to a good start. Giuseppe smiled. The men got right down to business and began discussing the purchase of the piece of land that appeared to be trash to most but that looked more like a golden opportunity to Giuseppe. Mr. Knight, impressed by Giuseppe, agreed to sell the land to him for only enough money to cover the back taxes on the property. He was not interested in making any profit on the land. This was fortunate for Giuseppe, and he felt an overwhelming sense of excitement.

The final sale went quickly and smoothly. The transaction was concluded at the company's headquarters in Providence, and Giuseppe Rossi was now the proud owner of his own land.

In the summer of 1911, Giuseppe was working nearly seven days a week to get ahead. It was difficult to find the time needed to clear his newly purchased land. Although his father posted signs like Private Property and Do Not Dump Trash Here, local residents continued dropping waste onto the land—mostly believing it was owned by the city. The harder Giuseppe worked to clear the land, the more trash was dumped. Some locals came by and taunted Giuseppe. He chased after one of them. The young men were too quick on their feet and scattered before Giuseppe could get his hands on them. Giuseppe became discouraged. Working eleven-hour days at the mill, then clearing land for several hours and raising a family took a lot out of him. He certainly was not as young as he used to be, he thought.

One Sunday while at Sacred Heart Church with Vincenza, Giuseppe asked Father Tirrochi to announce to his parishioners that he now owned the land near the cement bridge on East Avenue and that it was no longer a place to dump trash. As they left the church after services, people of the small village were whispering and pointing at Giuseppe and Vincenza. Some began to laugh as the couple walked by them. But over the next few weeks, the trash dumping subsided, and Giuseppe and his father were able to make considerable progress in clearing the land.

It was around this time that Vincenza learned that she was pregnant with another child. Giuseppe was excited for an addition to his family, but he felt more pressure than ever to finish clearing the entire property to build a home for his growing family.

In the fall of 1911, just as things were looking up for the Rossi family, Vincenza received a letter from her mother containing some disturbing news from Italy.

10 THE CONTRACTOR

Spring of 2001 was hectic for me. I was working many hours, and I found myself on the road more so than with past construction projects. Some of these projects lasted a few days—others were six to eight weeks. I decided to purchase a new laptop to correspond with my customers and keep financial records. When the opportunity presented itself, I conducted research online to find more clues about my grandfather's life and his invention.

My contracting business began to slow down in August—nearly to a halt—as commercial construction projects were becoming scarce. For many days, I found myself at home with no work lined up. This was the first time in ten years as a self-employed contractor that I was concerned about lack of work. After a few days passing, however, I received a call from my close friend Tim offering work on an estate settlement. I jumped at the opportunity, and he was excited to have someone at the site he could trust. We began the project in the first week of September.

The two-hour commute did not dampen my enthusiasm at all. The property was located in Torrance, California, high on a hill overlooking the valley. It was a small two-bedroom, one-bath home with a large backyard and patio from the nineteen fifties. Very little upkeep or maintenance had been performed inside of the home over the years; however, the outside had recently received a fresh coat of paint.

Tim and I dug into renovating the house. We removed everything from the home including furniture, appliances, and carpeting. We then painted everything and installed new carpet and the latest, sparkling bathroom fixtures. We cleaned the kitchen cabinets and sprayed the ceramic-tile countertops, shower walls, and bathtub with epoxy for a newer look. It would be a complete transformation by the time we finished. There was a feeling of pride while making progress on a job like this. The idea of revitalizing this home that had been neglected for so long felt like an accomplishment.

Then, in the second week of the project, a catastrophic event took place.

41

11 NEWS OF WAR FROM ITALY

Vincenza read the letter from her mother in disbelief.

September 19, 1911

Dearest Vincenza,

Our homeland has gone to war. On September 17, 1911, our armies were sent into battle in Tripoli and Cyrenaica in North Africa. Your cousins Alberic and Biagio have received letters from the government telling them to join the army by the beginning of next year or be sent to jail. I cannot believe this is happening; these boys do not have a mean bone in their bodies...

Vincenza put the letter down, unable to finish. She was sobbing heavily when her husband came into the room.

"Mama, are you not well?" he asked. "What is wrong? Is it the baby?"

"No, Papa, it's not the baby. It's this letter I got from my mother."

Vincenza resolved to pick up the letter herself and read it again in its entirety to Giuseppe. As he listened to his wife, Giuseppe tried not to show emotion because he knew that would upset her even more. But Giuseppe couldn't hold back—he loved Alberic and Biagio like brothers, and his eyes filled with tears. Giuseppe comforted his wife and helped her lie down to rest. When she fell asleep, he left the apartment to go visit with his father.

The news about Alberic and Biagio surprised Augustino and deeply upset him. "I know how you feel about these boys, son, but they must do as the government has asked them to do. It is their duty." There was a pause; Augustino was looking into his son's eyes and read his mind.

"Then it is my duty as well, Papa," Giuseppe said.

Augustino grabbed his son, put his arms around him, and gave him a bear-like hug. "I love you, son. Do as you feel you must."

And the decision was made.

On an early October morning of 1911, twenty-six-year-old Giuseppe hugged and kissed his emotional family good-bye. Vincenza promised Giuseppe that she would not cry, but she could not control herself and tears began flowing. After all, what kind of wife could stand to watch her husband leave for war?

Giuseppe Rossi

Giuseppe left his parents, his pregnant wife, and their three-year-old daughter. As he crossed the ramp onto the ship's entrance, he held his head high and did not turn around. He could not bear to.

It was with equal emotion that Alberic, Biagio, and the Di Domenici family met up with Giuseppe at the Campobasso train station upon his arrival. When they arrived back at the Di Domenicis', the family enjoyed a meal fit for kings. They ate, they laughed, and they drank copious amounts of red wine. It was a real family reunion. Although Giuseppe already missed his family in America, he felt at home in Italy.

Two days later, Giuseppe, Alberic, and Biagio were in the Military Affairs office to enlist in the Italian Army. The enlisting officer was so happy the three men enlisted together, voluntarily, that he agreed to place them in the same unit. And because they had volunteered, their tour of duty in the army would be limited to twenty-four months. Giuseppe realized he would be home in time for his second child's second birthday.

The men were stripped of their possessions and given two uniforms each. After two weeks of basic training, they were transported to North Africa with only a rifle, side arm, ammunition, helmet, canteen, and bed roll.

By the third week of January in 1912, Alberic, Biagio, and Giuseppe found themselves loading onto a transport ship in route to the port of Tripoli. Libyan freedom fighters began attacking their ship before the first wave of soldiers and supplies were able to disembark. The trio stayed within the port area for weeks as their ship and other arriving vessels needed to be unloaded of men and supplies. The men supplied security for the port, standing guard to the point of exhaustion.

A month later, a high-ranking Italian officer learned that Alberic and Biagio were brothers and that Giuseppe was related by marriage to their cousin. He separated the trio to cut the potential losses to one family. This enraged the men. Giuseppe understood, but he was adamant about the trio staying together. He later was sent to the brig for one day for talking back to a ranking officer for saying how he felt. Then he was reassigned to an ordinance and heavy artillery unit.

Alberic and Biagio were separated and sent to other base camps. There they would provide security and dig burial pits to lay their fellow soldiers to rest. On one occasion, during June 1913, the trio united again after nearly sixteen months of separation. The war had taken a visible toll on each of them. Seeing each other, however, raised the men's spirits. They found a café to spend some brief time together and soon had to part ways again. The men shook hands and embraced—no departing words were spoken, and no tears were shed.

In the latter part of their tour of duty, both Alberic and Biagio were sent to a large concentration camp where they provided security over men, women, and child prisoners. Considered light duty work, the post was where soldiers finished their tour of duty before being sent home. Sympathetic to the prisoners' plight, the brothers often secretly supplied them with extra food and blankets. They had also stopped carrying firearms as to not intimidate the prisoners any further. Both men grew too comfortable in their surroundings and believed they shared mutual respect with the prisoners. Ultimately, this assumption proved to be a fatal mistake.

On a cold, dark, wet October morning in 1913, the prisoners in the concentration camp began a well-planned uprising against their Italian military captors. The resulting death toll was high on both sides; many soldiers and prisoners were killed. Some prisoners escaped and were later captured. Many of the Italian soldiers had let their guard down over time and had not anticipated such an event. After all, they had fought in the war and were here to finish their tours of duty, or so they thought.

When the smoke cleared, the Italian soldiers removed their dead from the camps. The bodies of both Alberic and Biagio were found. They had been brutally clubbed and beaten to death by prisoners during the uprising. They'd had less than eight weeks left on their tour of duty.

The news would change Giuseppe's life forever.

World War I Italian Heavy Artillery

12 AMERICA ATTACKED

September 11, 2001, Tim and I stopped for an early breakfast at a nearby family restaurant before heading over to our worksite in Torrance. I had an omelet, and he inhaled some oatmeal and French toast.

At the house renovation site, he began prepping the wood-framed windows for paint. I was replacing the light switches and plugs. We turned on a radio for some background noise; it usually had a bit of static between stations, but we did not seem to notice. We took a break around noon; Tim took my truck to pick up some food from a nearby fast food restaurant. He didn't mind going, and he never allowed me to pay for food. I kept on working until he returned. I thought it was a pretty good deal.

That day, though, Tim fell from a stepladder in the backyard while cleaning a large picture window. Lucky for him, he landed in the bushes and got just a few scratches, a bruised forearm, and a sprained wrist. He was angry, and it did not help that I was teasing him and accusing him of "falling down on the job."

"Jesus, Tim, if you get hurt, who is going to get me my lunch?" I asked him laughingly.

"That's great," he said. "I'm bleeding and all you care about is your stomach!"

We both laughed and headed for the garage to the cooler full of cold bottled water.

Tim opened the door to get into the truck. Despite the aches, pain, and bleeding, he was still going to pick up lunch.

Leaving the driveway, Tim nearly backed into Mike, the neighbor from across the street. Mike had purchased some furniture from the estate we were working on, so we knew him rather well. Tim and I looked at each other thinking that maybe he'd changed his mind about the furniture. We had delivered it just the day before and had pushed it up to the second floor. We did not want to pick it up ever again—it was heavy stuff.

With his arms and hands waving in the air, Mike asked, seemingly out of breath, "Have you heard the news? Have you been listening?"

I could tell that Mike was excited. "No," Tim replied. "We've been working in the house."

"We've been attacked! First one plane, then another."

"What? Where?"

"New York City," Mike said. "First one plane, then another. They smashed into two skyscrapers and exploded. They think it's terrorists!

"We're being fucking attacked on our own soil. I can't believe this shit! They smashed another plane into the Pentagon," Mike continued.

Spit was flying from his mouth, and his face was glowing red.

I could not believe what I was hearing. Surely, he must have the facts wrong. How could this be true? How could this possibly happen?

"The FAA stopped all flight operations at all airports throughout the United States. Have you noticed how fucking quiet—"

Just then, two United States Air Force jets flew by, side by side, heading toward LA.

"You see? You see this fucking shit? They're probably attacking LA!" Mike yelled as he turned and headed back toward his house. Waving his arm overhead, he called out, "Come over and see it on TV if you'd like to." He walked quickly to his front door.

Tim and I looked at each other in disbelief. "This can't be happening," he said. "I'm going to go get some lunch. I'll put the truck radio on to see what I can find out," he said and drove away, heading up the hill.

I stood there for a moment, still in disbelief. As I closed the garage door, I looked over the valley. Mike was right. There were *no* planes in the usually busy sky—we were working very close to the Torrance Airport. It was too quiet. Yet we hadn't noticed it until Mike came over and informed of us of the attack.

I suddenly got goose bumps on my arms and a sick feeling in my stomach. What if this *was* all true? What if we were being attacked? My two kids lived near Los Angeles.

I went back into the house and quickly began working on tuning the old, static-y radio. It was true, it was all true. I sat down on the floor, my back against the wall, and listened intently. They had not attacked LA, but everything that Mike had said was true. New York City and Washington had been attacked, and another plane had crashed in Pennsylvania, southeast of Pittsburgh.

As I listened, tears came to my eyes.

Why? Why is this happening? Who would do this?

I was alone, angry, afraid, and feeling vulnerable.

Tim returned a while later with burgers and soft drinks. We compared notes about what we'd heard on the radio. Fearing what other possible events might take place, Tim decided to call it a day early. We put our tools away, locked up the house, and headed for home, still listening to the news in disbelief. I tried calling my wife on my cell phone but could not get through. All lines were busy. It seemed to take forever to get home.

My wife was not home from work when I arrived, and I was becoming concerned. I watched the film clips of the devastating events that had taken place on TV. I could not believe my eyes. President Bush, speaking from the Barksdale Air Force Base in Louisiana, said that the US military was put on high alert around the world and that all appropriate security measures had been taken. I felt a little more at ease knowing that our armed forces were on the job.

My wife, who was an operating room nurse at a nearby hospital, finally made it home. She had been delayed due to late staff arrivals. I was relieved, but I still had not been able to contact my son or daughter. Later that evening we all connected. Everyone was safe.

Was it over now? Would there be more attacks?

Like everyone else, I was concerned for my family on both coasts.

If war were declared against the cowards who'd committed these crimes, would my son or daughter be drafted into the military?

Would the president ask for volunteers?

My son was an amazing drummer and aspiring rock star, only twenty-one with musical talent well beyond his years. My daughter had graduated college and was building a prominent career for herself.

I could not bear the thought of my son or daughter being put in harm's way.

13 NEVER TO RETURN

A superior officer approached Giuseppe and pulled him aside to talk with him. "I'm afraid I have some bad news for you, soldier," he said.

Giuseppe looked into the officer's eyes; a flash of thoughts passed through his mind. Suddenly he felt ill.

"Perhaps you should sit," the officer commanded.

Giuseppe sat down on a wooden crate of artillery shells.

The officer placed his hand on Giuseppe's shoulder. "Son, there was an uprising in the prison camps. The prisoners had homemade weapons, and…your two cousins were killed. We have buried their bodies with the other soldiers who died that day. I'm very sorry." He continued, "Because you have so few weeks left here, we are going to ship you back to the home-land where you will be safe. You will be discharged soon. I have known your cousins for some time now—they had told me all about you. They were good soldiers. They were good men. My condolences to you and your family."

Giuseppe was in shock and did not explain to the officer that Alberic and Biagio had been his wife's cousins. They might as well have been re-lated by blood anyway. The officer took a step backward, stood at attention, and saluted Giuseppe. Giuseppe immediately stood up and returned the salute. The men shook hands, and the officer and Giuseppe parted ways.

Giuseppe, feeling weak and turning pale white, fell back down onto the wooden artillery shell cases. Feeling sick to his stomach, he turned his head to the side and vomited. He became upset and angry with an over-whelming feeling of being alone in the world. He began to cry, hiding his face with his hands.

Why did this have to happen?

Why couldn't he have been there to protect them?

Why were they there to begin with?

He would be forever a changed man, angered by this war and the death of his wife's cousins and dear friends Alberic and Biagio.

Two days later, Giuseppe boarded a ship headed back to Italy where in a few weeks he would be honorably discharged from the army. He immediately went to the home of the Di Domenici family. Giuseppe expressed his deepest sympathies to Mr. and Mrs. Di Domenici as he held back his own tears. They both put their arms around Giuseppe and held him tightly and cried. Mrs. Di Domenici could see that Giuseppe was traumatized by the war and the death of her nephews.

"Please understand, Giuseppe. We don't blame you or hold you responsible for the deaths of our nephews," said Mrs. Di Domenici.

"You left your own family in America and traveled here to help protect our nephews, and for that we love and thank you," exclaimed Mr. Di Domenici.

Giuseppe was later taken to the train depot and then he boarded a ship in Naples, bound for the port of Providence.

He would never return to Italy.

14 POST 911

ays after the attack in New York City, I was informed by my mother in Rhode Island that I had lost a cousin whom I'd never met before. It turned out that he was a corporate senior vice president who had been attending a business meeting in the World Trade Center on the one hundredth floor of the north tower when one of the hijacked airplanes destroyed the building. He lived with his wife and three children in New Jersey. That morning he took the train into Manhattan.

Even though I had not known my cousin or his family, I could tell that my mother was deeply upset. Her voice quivered as she held back the tears to tell me the story. "He left for work early that morning. He didn't want to be late for his meeting in Manhattan," she said. "Before he left the house, he kissed his wife and children and told them that he would be home in time for dinner. He was so young," she continued.

Feeling sad and angered by this event and the aftermath, I could sense my mother's pain and tried to console her, but words over long distance telephone were not enough. I knew what my mother was thinking—this had hit too close to home.

15 WELCOME HOME

January 17, 1915, a cold clear winter afternoon, the transport ship from Italy arrived in the Port of Providence. As he prepared to disembark, Giuseppe peered over the side rail down onto the dock, and to his great surprise, he saw his entire family and a many of his good friends. Excitedly he grabbed his duffle bag and threw it over the handrail down onto the dock. Wearing his army issue uniform and a few days' growth on his face, he made his way quickly down the gangplank to the dock below.

Vincenza had not seen her husband for more than two years—to her he looked thin and battle worn. With tears flowing from her eyes, and cheering from family and friends, she ran to meet him at the end of the ship ramp. Dockworkers and passengers from the ship joined in the cheer: "Welcome home, soldier!" they yelled as Giuseppe and Vincenza embraced as if never to let go.

As family and friends got closer, Giuseppa, Giuseppe's mom, interrupted the couple by tapping her son on the shoulder. Giuseppe turned to her as she handed him the young boy she was carrying. "This is your son, Nicholas."

Giuseppe raised Nicholas above his head, and tears flowed from his eyes. Nicholas (nearly two years old) and his sister Maria Angelina (now seven years old) hugged their father. Giuseppe's father, mother, wife, and children embraced in an emotional reunion as Giuseppe's friends clapped and cheered. Giuseppe shook hands and hugged his friends—it was a hero's welcome, and for a few minutes he forgot about the war he had left behind.

Giuseppe's father, Augustino, had made special arrangements with the trolley authorities to have a special car exclusively carry the group of seventeen passengers. Before they left the dock, Giuseppe got down on all fours and kissed the ground. He was home.

Sandwiches, warm apple pie, and hot coffee were served during the fifty-minute trolley ride from Providence back to Warwick. An electric heater inside the trolley kept everyone toasty warm. "Papa, have you made any progress with the land?" Giuseppe asked his father.

Suddenly there was silence on the trolley. Augustino smiled at his son. "Yes I have made much progress with the land, my son. When you are rested, we can go by there, and you will see."

Trolley Stop, Natick, Rhode Island
Early 1900s

City of Providence, Rhode Island
Early 1900s

As he looked around, Giuseppe noticed that everyone in the trolley was smiling at him. "Great, Papa. I can't wait to see it," he said as he put his arm around his father's shoulder and hugged him.

Giuseppe slept that evening and the entire next day. Nicholas and Maria stayed at their grandparents' house so Giuseppe could rest. When he finally awoke, his beloved Vincenza was at his bedside.

"I must be dreaming. I must be dreaming," he said as he gazed at his lovely wife.

Without saying a word, Vincenza began to remove the layers of clothing that she was wearing. As she exposed her breasts, Giuseppe became intensely aroused, sat up at the edge of the bed, and put his arms around her waist. "If I'm dreaming I don't want to wake up," he said and kissed his wife's breasts.

Vincenza giggled and pushed her husband back down onto the bed. "Well, if you don't wake up soon, you are going to miss the best part!" she said as she removed the rest of her clothing. The couple made love for hours.

By early afternoon Giuseppe and Vincenza were dressed and on their way to Augustino and Giuseppa's house to pick up the children. Once there, Augustino offered to take his son to the property by the river. Vincenza decided to stay behind; it was cold outside, and Giuseppa was about to make dinner for the family.

"Go spend some time with your dad," she said as she gathered the children.

"Looks like it's you and me, son. Come on, I will drive us there," Augustino said with a little bit of boasting in his voice that made Giuseppe even more eager to see what his father had been up to on the property.

Augustino had acquired a used 1908 Model T Ford from his employer at a bargain price. Giuseppe was pleasantly surprised that his father had purchased an automobile. "Great looking Model T, Papa, but can you drive the damn thing?" Giuseppe kidded his father.

"Not really, but get in anyway," Augustino chuckled.

The land was only about a mile away, and the ride there was a cold one as the Model T was equipped with only a canvas roof. The temperature that day reached only the mid- to upper forties, and it looked as if rain or snow might be on the way.

As the car approached the recently completed East Avenue Bridge, Giuseppe could see his property, and he could not believe his eyes. Less than fifty feet from the bridge on the roadside edge of the property stood a small house. Augustino pulled into the driveway. "Welcome to your new home, son," he said with emotion in his voice.

Giuseppe stepped out of the car, his mouth wide open. He looked at the somewhat incomplete house and then back at his father. "But... how—?" He was completely surprised and unable to get the words out to express his emotions.

Augustino put his arm around his son's shoulder. "It's not a new house, son. It's actually not a house...it's a railroad ticket depot. The railroad had condemned this building and was about to tear it down—it came from just up the street on East Avenue. I bought the place from the railroad for just one dollar and paid to have it moved here! With your help, we can finish the rooms and you can move your family in. There is a coal stove inside to keep you warm."

"I can't believe you did this for us, Papa! I don't know what to say." Giuseppe was emotional as he hugged his father. "Thank you, Papa, thank you," he said. He looked his father squarely in the eyes with both his hands on his father's shoulders. "Looks like your carpentry skills are better than your driving skills," he said, and both men laughed.

"Come, let me show you the inside. The cellar has a room too!" Augustino said eagerly. "Quickly before it gets too dark to see inside."

As they entered the building, Augustino excitedly rambled on about the house and the effort made getting it placed on the lot. Giuseppe could sense Augustino's pride from the enthusiastic manner in which he was telling his story. Almost immediately, he felt that the house should belong to his father not to himself, but he kept quiet and let his father continue the tour.

Augustino proudly showed off the little house to his son until it was so dark outside the men could no longer see.

That evening in the confines of their apartment, Giuseppe shared his feelings with Vincenza about the home his father had made for them. The couple agreed that Giuseppe would help his father finish the house and then hand the deed for the property over to his father. It was the right thing to do.

In the weeks that followed, Giuseppe visited his old employer Mr. Robert L. Knight and asked to be rehired. Unfortunately, there was not a full-time position open; however, Mr. Knight had an associate at a Providence firm called the American Screw Company.

Mr. Knight quickly drafted a letter for Giuseppe to take with him when he went to apply for a position. The trolley to Providence was nearby, and Giuseppe, with letter in hand, rode to Stevens Street and applied.

He was hired immediately as a millwright/fireman. The position was well suited for Giuseppe; he would maintain and repair the screw machines as well as the boiler and steam equipment. The city of Providence during that period had become the technological capital of the United States, anchoring companies such as Corliss Steam Engine, Nicholson File Company, Brown and Sharpe, Gorham Manufacturing Company, and the American Screw Company.

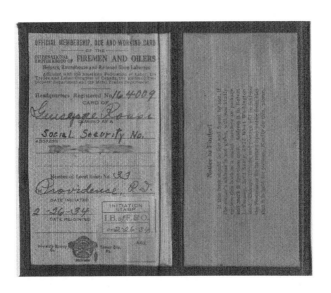

Robert Lippit Knight

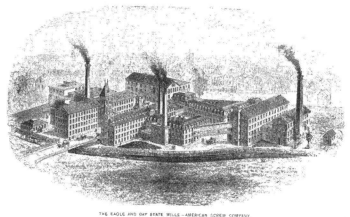

THE PROVIDENCE PLANTATIONS.

THE EAGLE AND BAY STATE MILLS – AMERICAN SCREW COMPANY.

American Screw Company

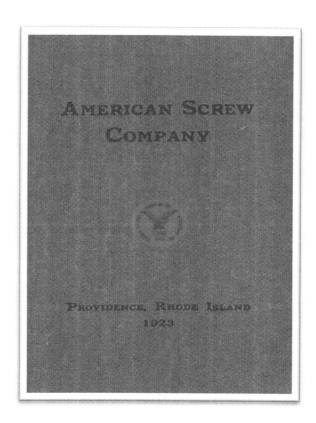

Giuseppe rode the trolley daily with other people who worked at these and other technologically advanced companies. He conversed with them and learned from them each day.

After he arrived home late in the afternoon of his first day of work with fresh cut flowers in his hand for his lovely wife and toys for the children, the family celebrated by going out to Vittorio's Italian restaurant for dinner. Late that evening while the children slept, Giuseppe and Vincenza celebrated the day's events in their own way, in the bedroom.

In April of 1915, Vincenza became pregnant with the couple's third child.

That same month the couple purchased a 100' by 150' lot in Warwick from the William B. Spencer Estates located on Riverdale Street. Giuseppe's dream was to build his own home for his growing family. It was a great location—distant enough from busy roads, on a corner lot close to the school, trolley, and fire station, and within one mile of his father's East Avenue home.

One afternoon, Giuseppe and his father were finishing the breezeway entrance of the East Avenue home when a well-dressed man approached and introduced himself as Henry Beron. "I have been watching the progress you men have been making on this building. It will make a nice home. I just moved into the house four doors up the street. Are you men going to be my neighbors?" he asked.

"Yes, my dad Augustino will be your neighbor. I am Giuseppe, and I will be building my own home around the corner on Riverdale Street."

"I am very pleased to meet you," said Henry as the men shook hands. "I have seen children here in the afternoon. Are they yours, Giuseppe?"

"Yes, my son and daughter play while my dad and I finish the house. Why do you ask?" Giuseppe replied.

"I own the ice cream shop on Main Street. You can't miss it—it has my name in big letters above the door," he boasted. "Bring your family by sometime. My children play in the lot behind the store while I work. They are about the same age as your children. Come on by, and I will serve up some ice cream!"

"Thank you, Henry. I will take you up on that offer," said Giuseppe.

They did not know it at that time, but this was the beginning of a lifelong friendship. Giuseppe had not told Henry how much he loved ice cream—he would become a steady customer. Henry and his brother Alexis would soon be helping Giuseppe build his new home on Riverdale Street on weeknights and Sunday mornings. Their children would play together in the yard and eat ice cream that Henry would bring from his store.

With the East Avenue home complete and his parents moved in, Giuseppe was able to commence construction of his new home on Riverdale Street. His plan was to excavate soil approximately eight feet deep (below the frost line) to construct a concrete foundation and create a basement. As he began digging, he discovered that the topsoil was a thin layer covering a deposit of sand and gravel. Taking a handful of moist sand from the ground and squeezing it in his fist, the sand held its ball-like shape. Giuseppe concluded that this was excellent material to mix with cement powder to build the foundation. He stockpiled the sand until the excavation was completed. With one-by-six boards nailed together to create concrete forms, the basement walls began to rise quickly. Giuseppe worked day and night mixing concrete in a steel tub.

Because the walls rose so quickly, Giuseppe decided that he would build the entire house out of concrete. He knew that his concrete mixture was strong; it would be indestructible, he thought, with low maintenance. Typically, a concrete foundation of a New England house would rise above the ground about twenty-four inches.

As Giuseppe continued to raise the concrete walls higher and higher, people from the neighborhood would come by to comment and stare at the concrete home construction in disbelief. "It's an ugly eyesore," some said. "It will crumble the first time we have a good frost," said others. On one occasion two men brought steel lawn chairs and cold bottled beers for themselves and sat at the edge of the property watching Giuseppe mix and pour the cement walls of his new home. Giuseppe ignored the men as they made jokes, laughed, and pointed at him. That did not bother him. However, he did get upset when he discovered that the men had brought cold beer for themselves and none for him.

With help from his father and several of his friends, including brothers Henry and Alexis Beron, Giuseppe was able to complete the construction of the first and second floors.

Henry L. Beron and Company

Before the roof could be completed, Giuseppe was forced to move into the house with his family. The lease at their apartment had ended, and the property owner would not extend it. Days after moving into the roofless home, it began to downpour rain. A neighbor, Mr. Paul Joyal, came to the family's aid by lending them several large canvasses to cover the top of the two-story structure.

The home was completed in late November 1915 before the harsh winter weather set in.

On Christmas Eve of 1915, Vincenza delivered a baby girl in her new home. They named the baby Christina Rossi.

16 THE MACHINE GUN

While in the army, Giuseppe had worked with a variety of weaponry and military equipment. Some things worked better than others in the field and in combat, but Giuseppe was often disappointed with the way many of the guns provided were functioning. After finishing the construction of his home, Giuseppe was thinking about other projects he could work on and was enjoying the space his new basement provided him for tinkering with tools and mechanical devices. He had a gift of imagination and the skills to create what came into his mind.

During the early winter months of 1916, Giuseppe began to work in the basement of his home on a project that he had thought about during his stint in the army. He began gathering supplies and the proper tools for creating a new weapon that could fire multiple rounds. The guns in the war had often jammed, and the trigger mechanisms were not useful for smooth, rapid fire. Utilizing some thick-walled boiler tubing and other machine parts that had been discarded from the factory where he worked, Giuseppe carefully assembled an operational, large-caliber machine gun.

Feeling confident with his work, Giuseppe took the homemade gun to the rear of his father's land to test fire it. After loading the ten-cylinder barrels with ammunition, Giuseppe stood behind the weapon, grabbed the crank handle on the right side, pointed the gun at some trees, and rotated the handle. Four rounds fired from the gun, hitting a three-inch diameter tree trunk and cutting the tree in half. With a big grin on his face, Giuseppe cranked off the remaining rounds at more of the trees with the same devastating results.

Giuseppe felt proud of what he'd crafted and was impressed that the gun functioned even better than he thought it would. He realized that what he'd created could be useful in battle, and he wanted to share this new invention with the American military.

After testing the gun a couple more times, Giuseppe visited the War Department office located in Providence. The duty officer listened intently as Giuseppe explained to him what he had built. The officer wrote down Giuseppe's address and place of work and told Giuseppe that someone would contact him.

On Monday of the following week, while at work, Giuseppe was summoned to the front office. A United States Army ordinance officer awaited Giuseppe's arrival. The officer introduced himself as Robert Meriden and told Giuseppe that he would like to see the machine gun that he had built. Giuseppe got permission to leave his work, and the two men drove in an army truck to the Rossi residence on Riverdale Street in Warwick.

Officer Meriden—in his early twenties and tall, thin, and prematurely balding—appeared and acted more mature than his years. With a wife and one child, a six-year-old son, at home, he loved being in the military and hoped to make a career of it. He had just purchased a home in the city of Warwick and was excited to begin raising a family.

Giuseppe retrieved his homemade gun from the basement and brought out a box of ammunition. He and Officer Meriden set up the machine gun in the corner of the yard. The army officer set up a paper bull's-eye target on a tree far from the house. With the gun loaded, Giuseppe got behind the gun, grabbed the crank, and was prepared to shoot it as he looked at the army officer for the go ahead. The officer stood to the right of Giuseppe with his left hand on Giuseppe's shoulder.

"All ready on the left," Meriden said as he looked to the left and then to the right. "All ready on the right." Finally he looked in the direction of the target. "All ready on the firing line." He tapped Giuseppe on the shoulder with the okay to fire.

In the time it took to rotate the handle of the gun, the paper target was obliterated with ten rounds of ammunition.

"That is amazing!" remarked Meriden as he walked toward the target area. "I'll replace the target. Point the weapon away from the target and reload it," he said firmly yet politely. Giuseppe complied.

Following the same procedure as before, Giuseppe fired the gun with the same effective results; only this time both men noted that the gun barrels were smoking, burning off oil residue that was on the steel. Again, Officer Meriden walked to the target and replaced it as Giuseppe reloaded the weapon.

The weapon was fired for the third time, again obliterating the paper target; however, the gun barrels were now glowing red from the heat produced.

The gun barrels were not the only thing glowing red. Giuseppe knew from his military experience that this was an unsafe situation. Firing more ammo could be dangerous as the barrels could explode from the barrel heat expansion.

"I am very sorry, Mr. Rossi, but we will need to stop the weapon test here," said Officer Meriden. "Your revolving gun fires well and is surprisingly accurate. It resembles a revolving gun built by Richard Gatlin in 1862—the original gun fired six rounds per revolution. You would need to refine this weapon so that it uses larger caliber ammunition and does not overheat. The gun would need to be lighter in weight and easier to move to be useful and accepted by the US military."

Giuseppe became quiet; he was disappointed and defeated. He had not heard of Richard Gatlin or the gun he'd invented. How could he make the gun lighter in weight when it already overheated the thick steel barrels? He put his head down as he listened to the army officer.

Officer Meriden could see the disappointment in Giuseppe's face.

"You are welcome to stop by the armory in Providence. I will show you pictures of several machine guns in books that we have there. The military is not really interested right now in another machine gun. I'm sorry to be the one to have to tell you this. I can see how much effort you've made here," said Meriden.

Giuseppe looked Officer Meriden in the eye but still said nothing as Meriden turned toward his army truck. Meriden stopped in his tracks and turned back toward Giuseppe. "What the military needs right now is a weapon that is lightweight...easy to move...can fly to where the enemy is hiding...and hit them...right in the fucking head," said Meriden jokingly to Giuseppe, trying to raise his spirits in a toying sort of way.

Surprised by Meriden's comment, who had acted professionally up until that point, Giuseppe began to laugh.

"I will work on it," replied Giuseppe. "Thank you for coming here today, Officer Meriden," yelled Giuseppe as Meriden drove away.

State Armory, Providence, Rhode Island

17 SUSPICIOUS ACTIVITY

Only days after the September 11, 2001, attack at the World Trade Center in New York, the news media began reporting that law enforcement agencies were arresting accomplices and suspects to this monumental crime. Pictures of the actual perpetrators were on television, and stories began to emerge of how they had lived as regular Americans and trained at US flight schools to carry out this act of terror. It seemed that anyone even remotely associated with being Muslim or of Middle Eastern descent was suddenly under surveillance, being detained, held for questioning, and investigated.

From 1995 to 2003, I worked full-time as a contract employee, essentially a contractor, for a company that was owned and operated by three business people who'd come from the Middle East. Although two of the individuals had obtained their US citizenship, one had not, and on the day of the attack, that individual's location was unknown. One of the men was actually in the Boston airport at the time the airplane was hijacked from that airport. The third was believed to be in Canada at the time of the attack.

Unfounded rumors had spread during that time that the entire Muslim community had been warned (secretly) that an event (attack) of large magnitude would take place in the United States on September 11; however, there was no mention of how or where.

The company I worked for was located in an affluent and well-manicured industrial business park complex. Ironically, in the office entrance, receptionist area hung a large framed print picture of the Twin Towers—the World Trade Center. The company was small with relatively few employees, but it catered to some of the largest and most technologically advanced semiconductor and government-contracted companies in the country.

It was a transitional period when the company was sold to a much larger corporation. The corporate buyer of the company requested the sellers stay with the company for a term of three years; this was standard operating procedure in this type of buyout. For this reason the sellers did not acquire the full amount of profit immediately from the sale; however, a large amount of cash must have been exchanged at the time of takeover, as the sellers purchased new homes, cars, and businesses.

The new corporate owner had a policy of not hiring contractors or contract employees. So in addition to hiring all the existing employees, I was offered a "Team Leader" position, which I gratefully accepted on January 21, 2002. I began my new position on February 4. Life was good, for a while at least.

The ramifications of the 911 attacks took their toll on businesses across the country.

We were no exception; the bottom soon fell out. Immediately no new business was coming in, no sales being generated. Employee layoffs began, beginning with our most experienced sales person, then an engineer contract writer, followed by a CAD draftsperson.

The remaining employees, engineers, and shop personnel including myself knew the end was near. The company was paying us to stand around; we simply had no work to do. But would such a large corporation close down a small company this soon after just buying it? In short—yes.

Meetings with corporate officers and my company's upper management took place during the second week of February. There was much tension in the air as rumors surfaced as to who would be laid off and who would stay employed. Since I was one of the highest paid field service technicians, I was convinced that I would be the first to go.

On the third Friday in February, all shop personnel including shipping and receiving were called into the conference room for a team meeting.

The general manager explained to us a series of "state of our business facts," which we employees already knew.

"Although it pains me to do so," he told us, "it is imperative for us to lay off all nonessential employees in order to keep the company alive through this tough period. We have decided that only one versatile, experienced, and capable person will remain with the company through this slow period to service our existing customers. The rest will receive layoffs effective immediately. We hope to have those persons who are laid off today return in a few weeks when business picks up again.

"Please do not say anything when I call the name of the person who will be staying on. That person may leave this room and wait outside until our business here has concluded."

The silence in the room at that moment was deafening as the general manager announced the name.

"Richard Rossi."

I stood motionless for a millisecond, feeling all eyes on me. Without making eye contact with the people I had worked with for years, I left the room.

In what seemed to be only moments later, they were all gone—fellow employees and friends that I had worked with for years. I was left standing in the huge shop warehouse alone. I was grateful to be the last man standing, to be employed. However, there were no customer service calls and there was no work.

Anyone else put in that position may have been thrilled to be the final remaining employee—I was not. It was then made clear to me that the seven laid-off employees would not actually be coming back.

Days passed and then weeks. I performed some minor customer service repairs and equipment installations. Whenever possible I would search for a new job on the Internet. Often when there were no new job listings, I would research information regarding my grandfather's invention on the company computer located in the warehouse.

Adolf Hitler, Benito Mussolini, Werner Von Braun, Buzz bomb, Doodlebug, patents, patent office etc., etc.—I focused on all the usual subjects related to my research. I sometimes considered who might be monitoring my Internet activity, but I continued the search nonetheless.

Meanwhile, a small laboratory within the company warehouse that had not been used much in the past was now being utilized by company scientists to conduct experiments relating to industrial waste treatment. In that area were glass and plastic bottles of chemicals with names I could not pronounce. Flammable storage cabinets held most but not all of these chemical ingredients. At the end of the day, many were left out on the table for use the next day.

Deliveries of new chemicals came almost daily, along with technologically advanced research materials and power supplies. It was my job to obtain and file Material Safety Data Sheets on all stored chemicals.

The delivery of those items were made by the same company and same person who had been making deliveries at our receiving door for years—a man in uniform with a large truck carrying packages. I cannot be more specific here; however, we knew each other on a first-name basis. Often in the past, he would tell tales of events that took place involving the customers on his delivery route. He paid attention to what was coming in and out of his truck each week.

For example, he had a customer that would receive large shipments of blue jeans for a local supplier. Additionally the customer would ship large boxes of blue jeans to Japan and other countries. He learned that the company was creating designer jeans by removing labels and reapplying counterfeit designer labels.

Knowing an operation like this was illegal, the deliveryman had notified his supervisor of his suspicions about the jeans. Law enforcement authorities were notified, and the counterfeit clothing company was soon shut down.

Now I was the object of his super sleuthing. He was quite observant and asked many questions. What had taken place in my company? Where had the other employees gone and when would they be back? What was the purpose of all the chemicals? Why weren't they stored in cabinets? What type of research was being conducted? On and on. He also casually commented on the Twin Towers picture in the front office and made comments about the owners of the company being foreigners from the Middle East.

The deliveryman's suspicions led to action.

The following morning at nine o'clock, local fire department officials made a surprise inspection of the facility. The general manager of my company led four inspectors on a tour of the facility. They inquired as to the use of the chemicals and made notation of what chemicals were on hand.

Two days after the inspection, the general manager received a letter from the fire department. It was an order to reduce the number of chemicals on hand and to provide proper storage facilities for the ones that would remain. Additionally, proper permits would need to be obtained from the city in order for the research to continue in the lab. My company had two weeks to comply.

That Friday afternoon at approximately 2:15 p.m., I noticed a police officer positioned in his black and white cruiser near the rear exit of our parking lot. He sat in his cruiser and pointed his radar gun toward oncoming traffic. He was still there when I left for home at 2:30 p.m.

This would be a regular sighting for weeks. A black and white in an industrial area, apparently looking for speeders.

Although these activities appeared suspicious or may have been coincidental, I must clarify that the men I was working for were highly respected business individuals. To my knowledge, they were never under suspicion nor detained for any reason—despite their country of origin, the inspections, and possible surveillance. The actual purpose of this information is to give the reader of my story some insight and understanding of how people who were not directly associated with or perhaps people who were formerly employed by my company, may have inadvertently perpetuated some future events to transpire.

With that said, I believe that the issues above instigated a number of unusual occurrences that began to take place around me—at work, home, and socially.

18 IF AT FIRST YOU DON'T SUCCEED

Frustrated and disappointed, Giuseppe sat staring at his failed invention. He had felt so close to making something that would be of great use. He contemplated for hours and hours how to make his revolving machine gun cool and operate properly—there was no simple solution.

He picked up the gun, as heavy as it was, and purposely struck it forcefully on the corner of the concrete house to damage the gun barrels so that no one could use the weapon. He then dug a deep hole in the backyard and buried the gun.

Giuseppe played with his children in the yard, planted a garden, and put up post structures that would eventually hold grape vines and provide a shaded sitting area. He suppressed the idea of becoming rich and famous - temporarily at least. He became busy at work. His knowledge and skills were in demand and were instrumental in the maintenance and continuity of work flowing out of his company.

Even with the admiration of his supervisors, Giuseppe earned a fair wage, but not as much as the millwrights who had more education. He knew he was more skilled, but they received more money and worked less. Yet he had a growing family and home to support, so he remained silent.

One late Saturday afternoon in September of 1916, Giuseppe was working part time in the Knight Textile mill. He had just completed repairs on a "Draper" textile loom. Although he was tired and ready to go home for the day, he requested the incoming night shift machine operator try out the loom to be certain it was operational.

Giuseppe leaned against a large wooden roof support timber and watched closely as the operator engaged the wheels, belts, and pulleys that powered the clattering, vibrating, rotating fabric-producing machine.

The operator replaced the shuttles that contained bobbins full of thread—known in the trade as "flying shuttles," they were made of rectangular hardwood with metal pointed caps on the ends. The center was hollow to hold the bobbin spool. The procedure was called "boxing the

70

shuttle." A feeler gauge on the machine would sense an empty bobbin and cause the shuttle to eject into the "shed." If the shuttle were not boxed properly, the device would eject over the shed area.

Suddenly an improperly boxed shuttle ejected itself from the machine. As if in slow motion, Giuseppe watched the ejected device fly gracefully from the machine through a multipane glass window to the outside of the mill. The machine operator was embarrassed that he had not boxed the shuttle properly. In all his years of experience, Giuseppe had not seen a shuttle fly that far. He walked to the outside of the mill to retrieve the device that should have been lying close to the building—or so he thought.

After minutes of searching, he found the shuttle in tall grass nearly seventeen feet from the building. Grinning from ear to ear, Giuseppe looked at the shuttle as if it were gold and thought to himself, what if this shuttle...*had wings?*

After going to church Sunday morning, Giuseppe sat in his kitchen with a pencil and began to sketch some ideas on paper. Inspired by the launched textile shuttle, he developed a new mission—to construct a military weapon like no other at that time, a "Flying Torpedo."

Vincenza could see the wheels turning in her husband's eyes and hear the excitement in his voice as he explained to her his new idea. It was a familiar sight, one that she loved. She would celebrate his new mission in the only ways that she could, first in the kitchen and later in the bedroom.

Samuel David Rossi was born in June 1917. Giuseppe and Vincenza would now have four children.

In the days and weeks that followed, Giuseppe gathered and assembled materials he thought could be used on his project and placed them in the basement of his home. Determined to be successful with his new endeavor, he enlisted the help of a few people he could trust and whom he'd known personally for many years. He wanted their work to be kept secret—not even close relatives or co-workers could know of their activity.

Alberto (Al) was a machinist at the American Screw Company. He had an extraordinary ability to fabricate almost anything from a block of steel. In his midthirties, Al had not served in the military and had a wife and three children at home.

Vittorio (Vito) was a metal forger and blacksmith by trade, but he was employed by the American Screw Company as a part-time millwright. Vito loved all things mechanical and had spent two years in the US Army. He was in his late forties and had a wife but no children.

John (Big John) was a boiler operator, friend, and former employee of the American Screw Company. He now worked the night shift several floors below ground at a bank in Providence, just around the corner from the American Screw Company. John's skills were many, but he especially enjoyed fine woodworking. In good health, yet old enough to retire, he chose to keep working. He and his wife Mary had no children.

Each of these men would be instrumental in helping Giuseppe create his vision of a powerful military weapon unlike any other at that time: a device that was portable, easy to assemble, and simple to operate. Offering the element of surprise from the sky, it would deliver precise devastation to distant enemy forces.

As construction of the prototype weapon progressed, Giuseppe went to the armory located at 176 Benefit Street in Providence and once again saw Officer Robert Meriden. Upon showing Meriden some simple drawings of the Flying Torpedo, Meriden agreed to visit Rossi's house the next day.

Meriden arrived promptly, viewed the device, and was very impressed. Using a sketchpad and pencil, he made detailed drawings of the weapon under construction—*for the sole purpose of explaining to his superiors the progress of the weapon*, he said.

Meriden continued to make drawings of the device throughout the completion of the project. He would return to the armory daily and brief an interested superior ranking officer, Major Armand Nollette.

Major Nollette retained the detailed drawings for review and then forwarded them to commanding officers in the War Department located in Washington, DC, unknown to Giuseppe. Meriden was apprehensive of his ranking officer's actions, but he remained silent. Meriden and Rossi had mutual respect; each had working knowledge and expertise with military ordinance, and they often spent time debating prototype construction options.

Occasionally, accompanied by his son, Robert Meriden Jr., Meriden would visit the Rossis and take his children to the Henry L. Beron Ice Cream Shoppe located on Main Street in Natick and buy ice cream for all.

As they became friends, Rossi deeply valued Meriden's opinions and ideas, but he would not give Meriden the satisfaction of agreeing with them. Unbeknownst to him, Meriden had been promised higher rank and a pay increase if he could assist Rossi in successfully completing the prototype weapon. Additionally, he was directed to advise Rossi not to attempt to sell his device outside of the United States.

War Department, Washington, DC

19 PARANOIA

At 2:30 p.m. my shift ended. I proceeded out of the rear parking lot exit in my Ford pick-up truck, making a complete stop adjacent to the police officer that was parked on the right side of the parking lot exit.

Looking left, I saw no oncoming traffic. As I pulled out to turn right, I looked in the direction of the police officer to get a glimpse of who he might be. The officer already had his eyes focused squarely on my face as if to gather all details. In that split-second glance, the expression I saw on the officer's face was that he had a preformed opinion of me that he knew exactly who I was.

Wow, what was that about? Perhaps I resemble some guy on a "Most Wanted" poster in the police station.

Judging by the look the officer gave me, I was certain that he would soon be behind me with lights flashing to pull me over and check me out. Glancing in my rearview mirror, the distance between us grew farther and farther as I rounded the corner and came to a red light. The traffic light turned green, and I proceeded one mile to the freeway—still no cop. I thought it must have been my imagination. What else could it be?

Continuing north on the 605 freeway, I occasionally looked in the rearview mirror, half expecting to see flashing police car lights, but there were none. I transitioned onto the 210 freeway heading east. As I merged into slow-moving traffic, I spotted a dark blue Ford Crown Victoria merge right behind me.

Perhaps not the black and white that my imagination had told me would be there, but a police-type vehicle with a low weighted-down profile and red and blue lights concealed within the grill.

Cautiously watching where I was going so as not to cause an accident or commit a traffic offense, I lost sight of the vehicle for a moment. Traffic halted briefly giving me an opportunity to do a 360-degree scan to locate the blue Ford, which was now located in my blind spot in the right rear portion of my pick-up truck.

For at least two miles I remained in the same traffic lane with the blue Crown Victoria on my right rear side; traffic progressed slowly as we approached the site of a vehicle accident located on the westbound side of the freeway.

Once past the accident site, traffic began to move freely. The Crown Victoria was now directly beside me on the right side of my truck. I grabbed my CD case and put into the player a music disc that my son Aaron and his band had recorded.

"Rock and roll, man!" I yelled at the blue car traveling beside me as I turned up the volume loud—loud enough for the cop inside the car to hear it, even though he had his windows closed.

A young man in his late twenties to early thirties wearing a white shirt and dark colored tie was looking straight ahead, not once looking in my direction. I finally was able to move left to a higher-speed lane on the freeway. The Crown Victoria moved left as well and reassumed the position directly parallel on my right side. With virtually open road in front of us, I maintained the speed limit of sixty-five miles per hour. The blue Ford remained on my right side slightly to the rear of my truck, shadowing me for the next fifteen to twenty miles. As we approached my exit off the 210 freeway, I slowed my vehicle slightly, allowing the blue Ford to come directly beside me. Now side by side, I stared at the person in the car, but he did not return the glance and continued looking straight ahead.

Quickly placing my right blinker on, I slowed my vehicle, got behind the Ford, and then banked right onto the exit ramp. "Have a good night, officer!" I yelled at the Crown Victoria (with my windows closed of course) as he continued easterly on the freeway.

So big deal. One cop looked at me funny, and another seemingly followed me home. Why was I being so dammed paranoid? Nothing happened—there were no black helicopters flying overhead, were there? Why do I feel singled out? Why do I have this feeling I'm being followed...

The distance from where I worked to my home was forty-eight miles. The average drive time was one hour and fifteen minutes. That afternoon because of the accident on the freeway, my drive time was two hours.

It's Friday! I am home safe; my wife will be home from work soon. We will go to dinner, see a movie—maybe I will get lucky! Okay, two out of three...

Just then the phone rang in the kitchen. I answered; my wife was calling home using her cell to let me know that she just left work and was— click, click, scratch, scratch, static, static.

"Hello, hello, can you hear me?" I asked my wife.

"Yes, I can hear you," she replied. "What happened to our connection?"

"Don't know! I'll talk to you when you get home!"

"Okay. Bye!" Scratch, scratch, static, static.

A short while later my wife, Jan, got home safely, and we decided to invite our friendly neighbors to join us for dinner at our mutually favorite Mexican restaurant located in the city of Pomona.

Sipping on soft drinks and coffee, my wife and neighbors began to laugh as I explained to them my afternoon experience. "First one cop... then another...now the damn phone!"

We all laughed and enjoyed our dinner. At the end of the day—it was funny.

What an idiot I am, I thought.

Bush-era surveillance went beyond wiretaps

JOHN MEYER
REPORTING FROM WASHINGTON

The Bush administration's post-Sept. 11 surveillance efforts went beyond the widely publicized warrantless wiretapping program of previous day, encompassing additional secretive activities that created "unprecedented" spying powers.

The report also raised new questions about how the Bush White House kept key Justice Department officials in the dark as it launched the surveillance program.

In a move that it described as "extraordinary and inappropriate," the report said the White House relied on a single, lower-level attorney in the Justice Department's Office of Legal Counsel for assessments about the programs' legality.

The attorney, John Yoo, a young George W. Bush appointee with close ties to the president's inner circle, wrote a series of memos blessing the program even though his superiors and most top officials remained uninformed about it.

The report was compiled at the request of Congress by five government agency watchdogs: the inspectors general of the Justice Department, Pentagon, CIA, Directorate of National Intelligence and National Security Agency.

It represents the most detailed public disclosure of the existence of secret surveillance efforts beyond the warrantless wiretapping program, saying the overall package of efforts came to be known in the Bush administration as the "President's Surveillance Program."

However, the report did not describe the other programs or explain how they worked.

"All of these activities were authorized in a single presidential authorization," the report said, referring to the warrantless wiretapping as a "terrorist surveillance program" and the [See Surveillance, Page A16]

Saturday morning and afternoon were filled with the usual domestic chores—cut the grass, trim the bushes, clean the pool, wash the vehicles, and, most importantly, take an afternoon power nap!

Saturday night we headed to LA to meet my daughter Alecia at a high-profile nightclub where my son and his band were playing.

I sometimes felt uncomfortable and out of place being around this group of young people—that is, until my son Aaron was on stage shredding on the drum set. The band had a huge number of followers who swirled and mashed in the mosh pit. It was great—such mayhem!

After a long night of listening to metal and watching the moshers, Sunday morning we awoke around ten. I retrieved the Sunday *LA Times* from the driveway, and my wife headed to the kitchen to start making cottage cheese pancakes, sausage, and fresh coffee. *I love it when she spoils me!*

Morning soon became afternoon; I was ready for a nap on the couch and proceeded to lie down. I was out cold in seconds, snoring, drooling, and content.

Suddenly the doorbell awakened me. As though I had awakened from a coma, I was somewhat disoriented and could not move. Our two cats had fallen asleep on me; Biscuit was stretched out on my hip, and Sophie, on the arm of the couch, had her front paws on my forehead.

Maybe they'll go away. Am I dreaming this?

I heard the bell again and glanced at my watch: 3:17 p.m.

Who can it be? Where is Jan? Why won't she answer the door? It must be Pete.

Pete was my neighbor. In his late eighties, he was a retired hospital chef. He loved to cook for his family and friends. He would often bring food or treats for us to enjoy.

I got my lazy self off the couch, walked quickly to the front door, and opened it. To my surprise there were three well-dressed people standing there. Unfortunately, for me, none of them were carrying freshly made food or treats.

Having just woken up, I stepped outside my front door feeling as if I had just crawled out of a duffle bag wearing a tee shirt, shorts, and white socks. I could feel pillow crease lines on my face.

Two of the men were very tall—one a thin, fair-skinned Caucasian with blonde hair and the other a well-groomed black man with wide shoulders. Both seemed to be in their midthirties, and they wore expensive well-tailored suits. The third was a young white man in his late teens wearing a black sport jacket, white shirt, and tie. All three were carrying pamphlets and Bibles.

"Hello. How can I help you?" I asked.

With his hand extended to me for a handshake, the tall white man standing to my right said, "Hello, I'm Kyle," and we shook hands. "This is Mike," he said as I shook hands with the black gentleman standing to my left side. "And this young man is Christopher," he said smiling proudly. I stepped forward to shake hands with the young man standing directly in front me.

The young Christopher was approximately my height, 5 feet 8 inches. We were dwarves compared to the two men he accompanied.

(Note: The real names of these men have been changed to protect their identity.)

In the street behind Christopher, my eyes caught a glimpse of my wife in her Ford Explorer pulling into our driveway as the garage door began to open. Simultaneously, I spotted the vehicle the trio had arrived in—a black Dodge Ram pick-up with a white camper shell.

Although it had no markings or colored lights that could be seen, I knew instantly that this was a police utility vehicle. If I had been wearing a smile on my face when I first shook hands with Christopher, it was now gone. For a brief moment, I became completely deaf to what Kyle was saying to me as my brain tried to reason why these men were at my house.

Releasing the handshake grip, I stepped back from Christopher; my eyes went from the black and white truck to Christopher's now worried face.

What do these guys want with me? Why are they here? Is this another coincidence? Am I being paranoid again? Is this because of where I work or because of my research on the computer? Are these people FBI, or local law enforcement...WHO ARE THEY?

Without missing a beat, Kyle got my attention again and continued. "We are Jehovah's Witnesses in your neighborhood today spreading the word of God. Do you believe in God, Richard?" he asked.

"Yes, I do. I'm Catholic...and how do you know my name? I didn't give it to you," I said calmly as the phone began to ring inside my house.

"Oh...aaah...we asked your neighbor whom we might find at home here...*they* gave us your name," responded Kyle in a matter of fact tone.

That was clever, but I'm not buying your bullshit.

I could hear the ruffling of plastic shopping bags coming from inside the house and my wife's voice as she answered the telephone. "Rich...telephone," she yelled from the kitchen.

Pretending that he did not hear my wife call to me, Kyle now had a pamphlet in his hand with a picture of the Twin Towers in New York City, just after the first plane had struck the building.

"What do you think would drive men to commit such a horrible act and how do you think we could prevent this from ever happening again?" he asked probingly.

Is this person for real? Do I look like a philosopher standing here in my shorts, white socks, and T-shirt? If I am being investigated, I had better be careful how I answer. What kind of a response was he looking for?

Yeah, I got just the thing. Let's go blow those guys up with a shitload of my grandfather's flying torpedoes. You know—the ones I have the plans for in my house. That's why you're here, isn't it? Is that what you want to hear, dickhead?

Taking the pamphlet from his hand, I looked down at the picture and then up directly into Kyle's blue eyes as he awaited my answer. I pointed at the exploding tower picture. "I have a cousin who died when the plane hit that tower. He was on the hundredth floor. He had gone there for a morning business meeting," I said emotionally.

Just then Mike, who had been standing in silence and looking like he would tackle me if I did something stupid, relaxed and leaned against the house. "My God, it even hit home here. We are very sorry to hear of your loss, Mr. Rossi," he said respectfully. "Did you know him well?" he asked.

"No, I didn't know him. However my mother told me of the devastating effect his death has had on our family members."

Why would Mike ask that particular question? Had he heard the conversation that I'd had with my mother on the phone days earlier? How did know and remember my last name?

"Rich...telephone...it's your brother," my wife called to me again.

20 PROTOTYPE TAKES FLIGHT

Early one Sunday morning in mid-September 1917, Giuseppe felt quite accomplished as he rolled a completed prototype weapon in a rusty steel wheelbarrow from the Rossi home, across Bald Hill Road, to an immense open field.

(Today this field is the home of the Rhode Island Mall formerly known as the Midland Mall, bordered by Routes 2, 113, and 295.)

Big John carried the "launch base" on his shoulder. A white three-rail, wood-board fence surrounded the property that was sometimes used to pasture cows and horses. Big John handed the torpedo prototype and launch base over the fence to Giuseppe who had already climbed over the fence.

As they looked out over the field, the land area to their left was nearly flat, but to the right toward East Avenue the land was substantially elevated. Tall grass and a few outcroppings of stone ledge made up the landscape.

"Let's go up the hill, Big John," Giuseppe commanded, pointing in the direction of higher ground.

"Yeah, let's get it high on the hill so we can watch it can roll down on its own," Big John laughed.

Hearts pounding and breathing heavily and perspiring from climbing up the grassy hill, both men were excited and laughing like schoolchildren.

"It sure as hell ain't gonna fly down," responded Giuseppe with a bellowing laugh.

"By the time we get to the top of this hill, I might not have enough energy to walk back down," replied Big John, exhausted but still laughing. "You may have to carry me!"

Reaching the summit of the expansive open field, the men sat down to rest. Looking across to the far side they wondered, could their homemade contraption fly that distance?

Big John helped Giuseppe place the torpedo onto the support saddle of the base and prepare it for launch.

Only a small amount of motor propellant (a slow-burning powder such as that employed in bombs and sky rockets) had been loaded to the propeller drive mechanism located at the rear of the torpedo. A spiral-wound tube containing this material was connected by a sleeve to the propeller drive shaft. A manually operated strike mechanism and firing cap enabled the burning of the propellant. The weapon was designed for an operator to pull back the trigger and release so as to strike the cap and ignite the powder in the spiral container. This started the propeller shaft and caused the tractor propeller to propel the torpedo into the air. The horizontal rudder was adjusted with a crank handle to set the desired altitude and direction; the device was now ready for launch.

The design was such that during actual wartime use of this device and with a predetermined length of travel of the torpedo, timed fuses on bombs, located beneath each wing, would ignite and thereby destroy the wings causing the fuselage of the torpedo to fall to the earth. Upon impact, the torpedo body that contained explosives would impose great destruction in the ranks of the enemy. However, this procedure was not tested on the torpedo's maiden voyage.

With the device now ready for its first-ever launch, Giuseppe made eye contact with Big John, his eyes filling with tears. Big John assumed it was the excitement of the moment that was making his friend well up with tears, but alas, it was not.

Giuseppe pulled back the firing trigger on the torpedo, looked up toward the heavens, and said, "This is for you, Alberic." Then he looked down toward the ground and with that Rossi sense of humor said, "And you too, Biagio!"

Giuseppe released the firing trigger, the hammer made contact to the firing powder, and a small puff of smoke arose from the mechanism. A hissing sound started up from the spiral propellant tubing, which had begun to heat up. The propeller was now whirling and quickly gaining momentum. Giuseppe and Big John held the torpedo firmly until the propeller was spinning with enough force to pull itself from their grip. The torpedo, still attached to the launch base, began to roll quickly downhill and away from its two pursuers, swatting a pathway through the tall grass with its sharp-edged propeller like a horizontal bladed mower. With a spray of freshly cut grass and weeds on their faces and in their eyes and mouths, Big John and Giuseppe chased the elusive speeding torpedo. Then suddenly the base of the torpedo dropped into a depression, and the torpedo left its base and became airborne, ascending to an approximate elevation of seventeen feet above the ground.

Giuseppe and Big John stopped in their tracks, their faces and clothing covered with grass and dirt, panting for air and sweating profusely as they stared wide-eyed at the amazing flight of the homemade airborne torpedo.

The flying torpedo flew successfully approximately three hundred yards that morning on a predetermined, minimal amount fuel supply.

Unknown to the inventor, it would also be the final flight of his device.

Waiting for Giuseppe and Big John at the fence was Robert Meriden, grinning from ear to ear. He had witnessed the maiden voyage of the device.

Robert grabbed Big John and Giuseppe and placed his arms around their shoulders. Together the threesome began to go round and round in a circle whooping and laughing with elation of the torpedo flight. The dizzy trio fell to the ground. Lying back quietly and resting for a few moments, almost in a trance, the three men each began to wonder how this event might forever change their lives.

Robert Meriden sat up first. "Giuseppe," he said loudly, "that was amazing, and it is the reason I am here to see you. I have some information for you to look at about getting your flying torpedo patented. I wrote to the patent office of Victor J. Evans in Washington, DC, and they sent me this booklet," he said as he handed the booklet to Giuseppe.

Glancing at the booklet's pages, Giuseppe then clenched his fist with his right hand. Meriden saw this, but before he could speak, Giuseppe swung and hit Meriden in the left arm. "Thanks, Meriden. You are a good man and a good friend."

Meriden, now sighing with relief that Giuseppe had not actually hurt him, continued, "I will be more than happy to help you as much as I can with that. Please, just let me know…"

Victor J. Evans Pamphlet

Later that evening, Giuseppe and his oldest child, Maria, looked over the pages of the patent information booklet. Giuseppe went to bed but could not sleep. He knew he needed to patent his invention and that it could cost him a great deal of money—which was scarce in most Natick households in those days.

The next morning, as he prepared Saturday morning breakfast for his family, Giuseppe announced to his wife and children that he would travel to Washington, DC, to obtain the patent. Vincenza was silent; she knew her husband and could hear the excitement in his voice. She wondered if he could handle impatient patent lawyers when he arrived there.

21 RHODE ISLAND EXPEDITION

ime passed and life's events had a way of robbing precious time I needed to work on this story. The enthusiasm to complete the work and research has always been there; however, the time to do so has not.

My pursuit of a career change and the failing health of close family members began taking precedence over my writing and exploring more about my grandfather and his invention.

While my immediate family was well, my older brother Jerry began having some major health issues. A decorated Vietnam War veteran, Jerry suffered from a number of postwar health issues. My concern for his well-being consumed my thoughts, and writing this story went to the back burner for a time.

In early 2003, I took advantage of some accumulated vacation time and flew back to Rhode Island with my daughter Alecia to visit my East Coast family members.

Leaving T.F. Green Airport en route to my mother's home in West Warwick, we took a slight detour and stopped at the site of the country's worst nightclub fire. After a pyrotechnic accident during a rock concert, The Station nightclub had burned nearly to the ground. When Alecia and I got to the site, the place had been cleared, and the plot of land was now a memorial to the one hundred people who had perished there. It was difficult for my daughter and me to hold back tears, even though we had not actually known anyone who died there. It was such a devastating tragedy for those families whose loved ones died or were injured the night of February 20, 2003.

Finally we arrived at my mom's house, and she was waiting on her front porch for us as we descended the steep hill to her small, white home—the house I'd grown up in. After some quick hugs and kisses, we jumped back into the car to go visit my brother who was in the hospital and about to undergo surgery.

My brother's doctors had advised him against this surgery because the risk was great due to his already impaired physical condition. The chances of him not waking up were fifty/fifty. Jerry knew of the risk and decided to move forward with the surgery—it needed to be done, he said. Jerry's wife, Marie, and daughter, Lysa, were there to support him, but it felt more as if they were there to say good-bye. There were many tears.

As visiting hours were coming to a close, I asked the family if I could speak with my brother alone. Everyone agreed and my family members left the room.

It was tough to hold back the tears. My brother, with his usual quick-witted manner, cracked a joke that made us both laugh.

"How's your Giuseppe book coming along?" Jerry asked.

He's about to go under the knife and he is asking me about my book.

"I haven't worked on it much lately. I need to do more digging," I replied.

"Did you ever find out where the original model went to? Have you checked the Smithsonian?"

"No, I spoke briefly with Uncle Nick, and I got some interesting information from him."

"There's a family secret there I suspect…"

"Huh! My thoughts exactly, but what is it?"

Jerry looked toward the hospital room door as if to verify that it was, in fact, closed. Then in a lower voice, he said, "I have never told anyone what I am about to tell you."

I leaned in closer, not sure what to expect about what he might say next.

"When I was a teenager, I went down to the basement of our house in West Warwick to see what Dad was doing. I knew he was in his workshop.

"As I walked towards him, I saw that he had a gun in his hand. Dad was startled when he looked up and saw me staring at the gun. He then yelled at me to go back upstairs.

"I had never seen Dad act that way before or even after that," Jerry said. "When he came upstairs afterward, he acted as though nothing had ever happened."

"What do you think happened?" I asked.

About this time the sedative, which had been administered to my brother, seemed to take effect. Jerry's speech was becoming slurred.

"I think they killed someone," he said as his eyes rolled and he began to lose consciousness.

In disbelief of what I was hearing, I asked him, "Who is 'they'? Who did they kill? What are you talking about?"

"The brothers, I think they killed someone."

22 TO WASHINGTON

With full support of his family, Giuseppe went to Washington accompanied by his wife's uncle, George Lancellotta, who would interpret and speak on Giuseppe's behalf. They boarded a train Sunday morning from the nearby Natick train station to Hartford, Connecticut, where they switched trains for Washington, DC. Giuseppe was carrying the disassembled prototype torpedo with its launching base wrapped in brown paper tied with white string. He also carried some food and a single bottle of red wine packed in cloth sacks by Vincenza and Angelina for their day-long journey.

Once the men arrived at the train station in DC, it was easy to hail a taxi and secure a nearby hotel for evening accomodations.

George had arranged with the taxi driver to pick them up again in the morning to take them to the Victor Building located on Main Street. As requested, the taxi driver arrived promptly at eight in the morning on Monday to retrieve the men and their parcels. Giuseppe and Uncle George arrived at the Victor Building in only a few minutes. It was an impressive new building bustling with people scurrying to get to work on time.

The Victor Building

Although both men were dressed well with white shirts, red ties, and black trousers, they could easily see that the men and women entering the building through the glass doors were dressed in very expensive suits and clothing. The Washington professionals' clothes were pressed to perfection, and the men and women wore the most stylish hats of the day. Giuseppe, feeling a bit intimidated, mustered his quick-witted humor and quietly said in Italian to George, "They probably wore the same clothes to church yesterday." The joke caught George off guard, and he laughed immediately and loud enough to catch the eyes of a few passing people.

Upon entering the busy lobby, George went directly to the ornate wood desk surrounded by beautiful green plants in the center of the lobby with a small sign on its glass top that said Information.

"May I help you, sir?" asked the young well-dressed and manicured woman behind the desk.

"Yes you can," answered George with a polite smile. "My nephew and I are here to see Mr. Victor Evans to file for a patent. Where may we find his office please?"

"The Patent Office is located on the top floor. Take any elevator," she said in a sweet voice, pointing to the elevator doors.

Giuseppe had often used large freight elevators in the mills; however, George had never ridden an elevator before and did not know what to expect.

They entered the elevator; an attendant operated the elevator controls. The elevator rose quickly causing George and Giuseppe to buckle slightly at the knees. The attendant grinned widely as he delivered the men to the sixth floor of the building.

Giuseppe and George stood quietly and patiently behind the counter, waiting to be acknowledged by the young well-dressed patent attorney who was intentionally ignoring the two men on the other side of the counter. The brown paper parcels they carried crunched and crackled as they stood trying—unsuccessfully—to hold the heavy prototype equipment silently.

"Excuse me, young man. May we please have some assistance?" George inquired loudly enough to get everyone's attention in the office.

Acting as though he was startled and with a look of having been annoyed by their presence, the young lawyer looked up and responded (knowing that other employees in the office were now watching him), "How may I help you, gentlemen?"

"We must speak with Mr. Victor Evans as quickly as possible. Can you direct us to his office?" George inquired hastily, as the young man was wasting his valuable time.

Patent Office Employees

"Do you have an appointment to see Mr. Evans?"

"No, I do not. I didn't know I needed one. Can you point to his office please?"

"What is this in regards to?" asked the young man who was now intentionally trying to aggravate George (and doing a good job of it).

Becoming impatient and glowing red in the face, George was ready to jump over the counter to pummel this guy when Giuseppe grabbed him by the shoulder and restrained him. "Remember what Vincenza told us before we left?" Giuseppe whispered and smiled.

Suddenly a well-dressed man in a crisply pressed suit appeared behind George and Giuseppe on *their* side of the counter.

"How may I help you, gentlemen?" he asked with his hand extended for a handshake. "I am Victor Evans," he said with a smile. "Welcome."

89

Victor J. Evans
Attorney

With a firm grip and some brief discovery questions, Mr. Evans again welcomed George and Giuseppe and invited them with their packages into his personal office.

Victor Justice Evans was a self-made millionaire. Born in Ohio in 1865, his family had moved to Washington when he was a young boy. He became skilled in the art of drafting, and this talent was instrumental in his success, as he had four patent offices throughout the United States. He had also become deeply interested in inventions related to aviation.

Private Office of Victor Evans

"You have obviously traveled a great distance to see me. Now let's see what you have to be patented." He began to help George and Giuseppe unwrap the prototype torpedo components.

"My, my…what do we have here? Giuseppe you *are* a very talented man," Mr. Evans said in amazement. "Have you tested it? Will it fly?"

George began to answer, but Mr. Evans interrupted.

"No, please, let Giuseppe speak for himself," he requested with his hand up in a motion to stop George.

"Yes, Mr. Evans. I built this model in my basement at night after work and Saturdays too," Giuseppe explained. "This is only a model, but I flew it in the field near where I live. That's why it's a little scraped up on the bottom side."

"I have friends at the War Department here in town that will be very interested to see this device of yours. I will ring them up and get them here as quickly as possible. Can you leave it with me for a few days?" Mr. Evans asked.

Giuseppe looked at George, and without saying a word, they both knew that the expense of staying in the city plus losing time from work at the factory was a hefty toll to bear.

Mr. Evans sensed the problem before a word could be spoken.

"Gentlemen, leave the prototype with me today and tomorrow. I will have my specifications staff disassemble it, review it, and sketch it. I will have people work on it around the clock to get it done quickly—I will create the drawings myself, if necessary. I will also arrange to have my driver take you to a hotel for the next few days. Do not worry about expenses. Charge your meals to the room. You will need to spend some time here explaining *exactly* how the device operates so we can properly write your patent. I will pay the expenses incurred—you can pay me another day. It's the least I can do for you both since my staff member treated you so poorly.

"I will also be sure to have my military friends from the War Department review it before you take it home. They may be very interested in your device. What do you think?"

Giuseppe was excited to hear the word "patent" come from Mr. Evans and his generous offer to help ease the burden of staying in DC. "Yes, we will stay. Thank you. I will come tomorrow afternoon to explain how the model works. Thank you for your hospitality, Mr. Evans," Giuseppe said with an emphatic voice. "Thank you!" He enthusiastically shook hands with Mr. Evans.

By early evening, the preliminary drawings of the prototype flying torpedo had been completed, and as he had promised, Mr. Evans's military guests from the War Department arrived at the patent office to view the device.

War Department, Washington, DC

Mr. Evans was completely surprised to learn that his military officer guests had already seen Giuseppe's prototype.

"Sorry, Victor. We've already seen this torpedo on paper, but it's great to see the actual prototype!" said Major Caparelli.

"We've had our ordinance officer, Robert Meriden, in the Providence office follow the construction progress of this prototype. We also have detailed field sketches already," said Sgt. Major McLaren, boastingly.

"Honestly, this is a fine working prototype model—one of the finest I have seen produced by a nonengineer. But...its flying capabilities are extremely limited, and it is technically unrefined. It is truly remarkable that Mr. Rossi was able to fly this device. However, it has no means of guidance and could potentially harm innocent people. It would require a great deal of engineering hours to achieve the results we are looking for, and that is a long-range pilotless aircraft with its destination completely and accurately controllable."

"Would you be willing to work with Mr. Rossi on improving his prototype?" asked Evans.

"Sorry, Victor," said McLaren. "We have other individuals we are working with."

With that answer, McLaren forever changed the future of Giuseppe Rossi and future generations of Rossis.

How would life be different today for our families had McLaren said yes?

The following day passed quickly as Giuseppe and George worked with the specifications and drafting departments in the patent office, finalizing necessary details of the project. Mr. Evans arrived later than normal and confined himself to working in his office, seemingly avoiding conversation.

Once the specifications had been completed, the prototype was re-assembled and repackaged for the trip home. Giuseppe and George were ready to hit the road as they headed toward the patent office exit door.

Before they could pull the door open, Mr. Evans emerged from his office to shake hands with the men and present them each a new shiny brass Victor J. Evans letter opener.

"Giuseppe, I have prepared an *Evidence of Invention* certificate for you to take home. We do not have a patent number for you at this time—that must come from the Patent Office across the street. This document will fully protect your invention until you receive your patent documents."

With a big grin on his face, Giuseppe accepted the document from Mr. Evans.

Uncle George was grateful for the document as well, but he had questions such as how much the remaining fees would total. They had already paid a required first payment of fifteen dollars. And when would the actual patent be recorded? George did not want to be rude or upset Giuseppe while he was obviously floating on a cloud, so he remained smiling quietly.

Giuseppe could barely speak as he again thanked Mr. Evans; he was overcome with feelings of self-accomplishment, pride, and joy. Knowing a United States patent would protect his invention was simply overwhelming.

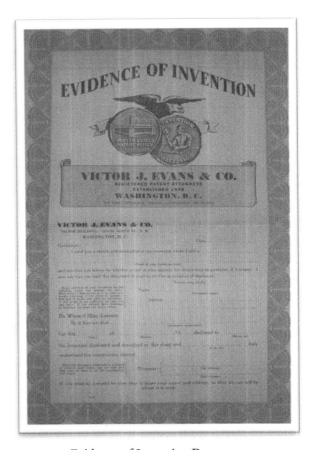

Evidence of Invention Document

23 SEARCH FOR INFORMATION

With only two days remaining in Rhode Island, my daughter decided she would visit with my mother in-law and her two uncles while I went to the Warwick Town Hall to research vital records. My goal was to research death records and possibly obtain a copy of my grandfather's death certificate.

Warwick Town Hall, Rhode Island

After filling out a form and showing identification, the attending clerk allowed me behind the counter and into an area that had large wood tables and seating for viewing the large handwritten official death records books. I knew the year that my grandfather had passed, and I was supplied a record book that contained the beginning of that year in order to locate the registered certificate number.

The pages of the record book had been well preserved, showing signs of wear only on the outer page edges. As I turned page after page I realized that the handwritten listings of deaths were chronological, not alphabetical. I turned the pages slowly, cautiously, and respectfully for those persons whose names were listed in each record. I was moved by the number of deaths that had occurred around the same time as my grandfather—so many in fact, that I became concerned that his passing may have not been officially recorded until I finally found the handwritten entry for Giuseppe Rossi.

I read the information several times—street name, wife's name, birthplace—to be certain I had actually found *my* grandfather's death record. The registered number was 37-36.

Although I was happy that I'd found this piece of tangible information of my grandfather, it was, after all, his death certificate, which made my heart drop a little.

Out of curiosity, I read the listing of the person whose death was recorded after my grandfather's. Registered number 37-37. I did not recognize that person's last name. Likewise, I also read the listing of the person recorded prior: registered number 37-35.

Registered No. 37-35
Date of Death.....................19...............
Name in Full...Maria Angelina Stabile
Date of Birth.......Age......
Place of Death, Street and Number........
Usual Residence...........
Sex..................Color.................
Single, Married, Divorced.......
Name of Husband or Wife..............

Birthplace, State or Country......Italy.........City.....Fornelli, Campobasso....
Father's Name.........*Giuseppe Rossi*......
Mother's Maiden Name....*Vincenza Rossi*......

What? Oh my God! That is just crazy!

I could not believe what I had found. My thoughts went rampant.

There is most definitely a family secret here. But what is it? What exactly happened here?

I immediately called my mother on my cell phone and informed her of my discovery at the Warwick Town Hall. To my amazement, she confirmed that this was in fact my father's sister, my grandfather's daughter; her married name was Stabile.

"I was a kid myself at the time this happened," she said, "but I remember when it happened. Your dad's sister and father died on the same day... hours apart in fact."

My grandfather, age fifty-two, and his first-born child died on the same day—February 17, 1937.

First off, I could not believe that this family tragedy had occurred and had never been mentioned. Secondly, until finding this death record, I had no idea that my dad had had a sister. Neither my dad nor his brothers ever mentioned their sister.

Maria Angelina Stabile left a husband and three children behind when she died; she was only twenty-eight years old.

I asked myself why and how this had happened. Even more strangely, the death certificates indicated that my grandfather and Maria had been taken to separate funeral homes for burial services. Maria was taken to John Di Orio & Sons, and Giuseppe was taken to Prata Undertaking Co.

Again, I asked myself...why?

24 HELP FROM FATHER TIRROCHI

The weekend following Giuseppe and George's return from Washington, DC, Giuseppe, Vincenza, George and Maria, Henry and Rosilda (Rose) Beron, and Robert Meriden, along with all the family members, held a celebration to honor Giuseppe's accomplishment.

The men did all the preparation and cooking. Giuseppe proudly presented wine that he had made with his own wine press. Tables were set up separately for the children so the adults could talk, but a close eye was kept on the little ones.

There was pasta with olive oil, salad with garden-fresh tomatoes, green and red peppers, homemade sausage, mushrooms, and olives. There was fresh-baked Italian bread loaves and sliced homemade mozzarella cheese, and, of course, fresh olive oil for dipping, drizzling, and pouring over everything. It was a special day with a comfortable temperature, great food, and smooth wine from the Rossi wine cellar. Ice cream for the children and, yes, cigars for the men—both compliments of Henry and Rose Beron.

The children tossed horseshoes or took turns riding the only bicycle in the family, which belonged to Nicholas. The women talked; the men laughed, drank wine, smoked cigars, and told war stories into late evening.

The celebrations soon ended, though. Giuseppe became concerned as several months passed, and no correspondence from the patent law office of Victor J. Evans had arrived. He simply did not think the patent process would take this much time. After all, the patent lawyer's office was across the street from the *actual* Patent Office.

On Sunday morning following mass at Sacred Heart church in Natick, Father Achille Tirocchi was saying good-bye to his parishioners on the steps just outside the front entrance to the church. Giuseppe, Vincenza, and the children all said good-bye to Father Tirocchi and shook his outreached hands.

Father Achille Tirocchi

Father Tirocchi had learned of Giuseppe's visit to Washington and asked him about it. A conversation ensued that led Father Tirocchi to offer to write a letter to the patent lawyer on Giuseppe's behalf. An inquiry as to when the actual patent might arrive was sent promptly to Washington, DC. It seemed that only a few days passed before a response was received at the Rossi residence.

A two-page letter with a return envelope arrived from Victor J. Evans's office stating in short that Giuseppe's invention was in fact patentable— however at an additional cost of $175.00, which must be sent to cover additional expenses as quickly as possible.

Giuseppe did not show any emotion after reading the letter; in fact, he was surprised the amount requested was not higher. He was accustomed to seeing invoices at the mill for machinery tooling that was far more expensive.

Nonetheless, this was a sizeable sum for the family man and sole provider to shell out, but he was so close to fulfilling a dream.

Giuseppe somehow tightened his belt and had the full amount requested telegraphed to Washington only a few days after receiving the letter. Now, for Giuseppe, the most difficult aspect of this whole process would begin—waiting.

LAW OFFICES OF
VICTOR J. EVANS & CO.
LARGEST PATENT FIRM ON THE WORLD
Solicitors of
AMERICAN & FOREIGN PATENTS.
TRADE MARKS & COPYRIGHTS

WASHINGTON, D.C.

MAIN OFFICE
THE VICTOR BUILDING
724-726 NINTH ST. N.W.
CORNER NINTH & STREET PARK.

Sept. 17, 1917

Mr. G. Rossi
20 Baker St.
Natick, R.I.

In re: Aerial Torpedoes

Dear Sir,

We have completed an investigation of the Patent Office Records in connection with the above entitled invention, and we are pleased to advise you that a favorable report has been rendered by us; that no similar such inventions with specific purpose as your invention have been registered, yours appears to be the first of record.

If you wish to proceed (recommended) with this filing application the order must be passed to our Preparation Force.

The minimum cost of a patent for an invention through our firm is $45.00. Our records indicate that you have made an initial first payment of $15.00 which covers the cost of preparing the application.

A second payment of $30.00 is required to cover the first Government fee, $15; the remainder of the attorneys' fee, $10, and $5, the fee for a sheet of official drawings.

---

2 G. Rossi,

A third payment of $20.00 covers the final Government fee to issue the patent. It may be sent six months after notice of allowance is received. This notice generally comes to hand three to eight months after the papers are placed in the Patent Office.

Cost to Apply: The cost to make application for a U.S. Patent for a simple invention is thus but $45, which may be made in two payments, the first of which is but $15.

Your invention will require additional sheets of official drawings and specifications for applications, to expedite the allowance of an application by the Patent Office examiners, $45.

Additional cost incurred during your visit to our Washington office included hotel and meal accommodations for two persons, $55.

Our charges are based entirely on the amount of work involved in the case; our charges will positively be as low as is consistent with the skillful preparation and prosecution and the proper protection of the invention.

How to Send Money:
In urgent cases where it is desirable to save time, remittances can be telegraphed. This form of remittance is especially desirable in cases where the time limit for the payment of the final Government fee is about to expire, or where the time is limited in which to secure valid foreign patents.
Do not send currency unless by registered mail or express. You can also remit by bank draft, post office or express money order, express or registered package or certified check.

Very truly yours,

VICTOR J. EVANS & CO.
BY. Arthur L. Evans

Immediately after Evans's office in Washington received and acknowledged Giuseppe's payment in full, documents began to arrive at the Rossi household. After several correspondence letters—amendments, alterations of device description, application and original drawing modifications completed—more than one year had passed. Finally, an official Patent Office document arrived for Giuseppe to sign and return.

Vincenza's Uncle George, who was also a Notary Public, witnessed Giuseppe sign an "Oath" document on August 9, 1918.

A document with the heading PETITION at the top and labeled To the Commissioner of Patents was sent to Giuseppe to affix his signature, which he did on August 24, 1918.

The document gave attorney Victor J. Evans of Washington, DC, "power of attorney" to make substitution and revocation, make alterations and amendments therein, and to transact all business in the US Patent Office regarding the Aerial Torpedo.

The document indicates that a fee of fifteen dollars was received on November 9, 1918, and recorded on November 12, 1918.

Months later, on February 27, 1919, Giuseppe again signed an oath stating that he was a "Naturalized Citizen of the United States" swearing that he had no prior knowledge of any knowledge of anyone having invented a similar device and that he was the original, first, and sole inventor. The document was witnessed and signed by Roscoe N. Lawton, Notary Public.

Giuseppe had already signed a similar document earlier on August 9, 1918. It was assumed that because George was the notary and a family relative, the document needed to be re-signed with a different notary.

George and Giuseppe began to believe that a deliberate effort was being made to delay the official patent of this device. It was taking too long to accomplish—and why did the oath ask if he had prior knowledge for more than two years of this device in the United States or in a foreign country? If he had, would he have tried to duplicate and patent it? Perhaps the real reason for the oath signing was to learn if the military had information leaks.

The patent application was finally submitted to the Patent Office and was filed and recorded on November 9, 1918.

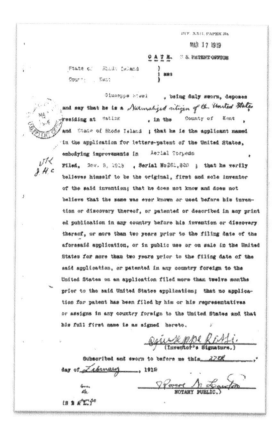

Unknown to Giuseppe, in September of 1916, father and son engineers Elmer and Lawrence Sperry—who were secretly working with the US Navy—filed a patent for an aerial torpedo design equipped with a gyrostabilizer to keep the aircraft level, an automatic steering gyro to keep the aircraft on a preset heading, and a barometer to indicate cruise altitude, causing the aircraft to level off. It also had an engine revolution counter to determine when the aircraft should cut power and dive into its target. The Naval Consulting Board then approved Sperry's aerial torpedo project and awarded the Sperry Gyroscope Company a $200,000 contract to build such a weapon.

Ultimately, the missile's "lack of progress" coupled with declining funds led the navy to cancel all efforts on the torpedo in 1922.

Elmer Ambrose Sperry

The Navy-Sperry Flying Bomb

At approximately the same time, the US Army secretly hired engineer, inventor, and scientist Charles F. Kettering (inventor of the automobile self-starter) to develop a "flying bomb."

Kettering formed a team consisting of his company, Dayton Metal Products (control systems), Elmer Sperry (gyroscopes), S.E. Votey of Aeolian Player Piano (pneumatic controls), Orville Wright of Dayton Wright Airplane (airframe), and C. H. Willis, Henry Ford's chief engineer (engine).

The device became known as the "Kettering Bug," although its official name was the "Liberty Eagle."

The army ordered twenty-five "Bugs" on January 25, 1918, from the Dayton Metal Products Company.

From September 26 to October 28, 1919, the army attempted fourteen test flights. Five Bugs crashed on or immediately after launching. While a few flight tests were successful, most ended in failure. The Kettering Bug project ran from April 1917 to March 1920 at a cost of $275,000.

Giuseppe wasn't aware of any of these inventors or of any of the work they had done on aerial torpedoes.

Charles Franklin Kettering

The Army-Kettering "Bug"

25 UNITED STATES PATENT

The first week of July 1919 was indeed a time to celebrate not only the Fourth of July, but also Giuseppe's finally receiving a document package from the United States Patent Office.

The package contained mechanical drawings of his aerial torpedo and several pages of descriptive language detailing the operation and construction of the device. Additional sets of drawings were also included.

Giuseppe immediately contacted Robert Meriden to give him the good news and to discuss what the next step should be to try to sell this invention to the United States military.

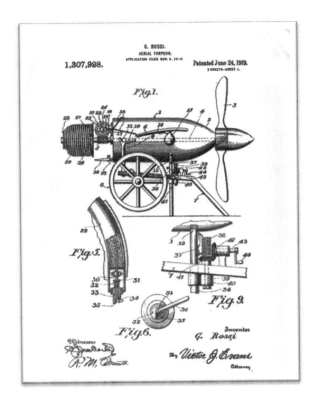

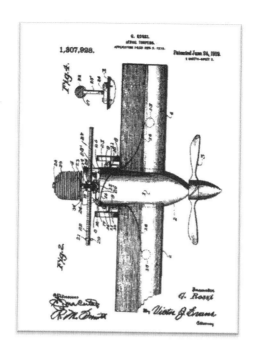

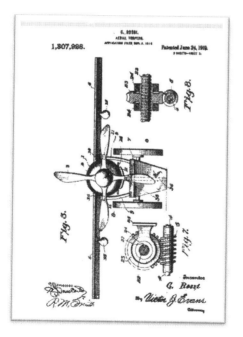

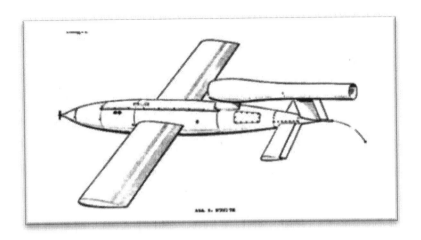

Could this weapon have been conceived from Rossi's aerial torpedo years after his death?

Hitler's V1 Aerial Rocket

26 FACTS FROM NICHOLAS

My daughter, Alecia, and I agreed that it was nice to have been able to visit family in Rhode Island, but it was now time to get back to California, our family, and work.

I was perplexed by what I had discovered at the Warwick Town Hall and discussed it with my mother via cell phone. She had always been interested in the progress I was making with my grandfather's story and the process of discovering new information about the past. She suggested that I contact my dad's brother Nicholas (Uncle Nick), the oldest surviving member of the Giuseppe Rossi family. Mom supplied me a phone number, and I was anxious to call.

On a Sunday morning, mindful of the three-hour time difference between Rhode Island and California, I called Uncle Nick, who was approximately ninety years old. It was late morning Rhode Island time.

To my surprise, he answered the phone immediately. At first he was unsure whether or not to speak to me. I had not seen my uncle since my dad's funeral ten years prior.

Once he was assured I was who I said I was, Uncle Nick briefly provided me some facts about the Rossi family that—up until that time—I had been completely unaware of. When I asked him, "What happened to the torpedo?" he replied that it had "disappeared." Our conversation terminated shortly thereafter, and I was still left with many unanswered questions.

27 TRAGEDY STRIKES HOME

obert Meriden sent copies of the Rossi flying torpedo to both the army and navy ordinance departments for review.

Response letters received at the Rossi household in early March 1920 revealed that the United States military had "no use for the device."

A disappointed Giuseppe allowed his friend Robert Meriden to read the letters. Officer Meriden showed no emotion as his read the letters. Wary of what Giuseppe might be thinking, he instead commanded Giuseppe—in a military tone of voice, one soldier to another—not to try to sell the device outside of the United States.

"We can try to find a military weapons contractor based in the United States to purchase your device," Meriden suggested. "I will personally see to it myself!"

Giuseppe reluctantly agreed; the men shook hands and parted ways once again.

It was a miserably cold and difficult winter, and it was far from being over. The Rossi home had an inadequate steam heating system boiler and only two radiators, one on the first floor and one on the second. During the winter months the boiler seemingly ran day and night.

It was a pleasure at times in the cold winter to be awoken in the middle of the night to the distinct hissing of steam coming from the relief valve of the radiator. It meant that heat was on its way to the gray metal warming fixture in the hallway at the top of the staircase.

Giuseppe had to keep a mindful eye on the temperamental boiler or it could fail. The tank within the boiler that required water to produce steam was in constant need of filling. The only source of water in the house at that time was a hand pump in the kitchen; the sink drained into a pipe, which went through the concrete wall of the house to the outside. (There were no sewers at that time.)

As the winter months carried on, April of 1920 brought a tragic event to the Rossi family. Christina, who had been ill with cold-like symptoms, developed a high-temperature fever and chills and began coughing up bloodstained sputum.

Vincenza kept Christina warm and as comfortable as possible until Giuseppe arrived home from work each evening. One night, around five thirty, Giuseppe arrived home, and when he took one look at Christina, who now had a bluish color in the face, he wrapped her in blankets and headed out the door. Vincenza stayed at home with the other children. The roads were icy that evening, and the closest hospital was in the city of Providence. Giuseppe opted to take the trolley to Providence—it would be heated and was the quickest, safest, most reliable way to travel to the Rhode Island Hospital.

Rhode Island Hospital, Providence

Christina began to hemorrhage from her ears only minutes away from the help she desperately needed. She then succumbed to her illness in Giuseppe's arms. Tears poured from Giuseppe's eyes as he sat alone on the trolley; his five-year-old baby girl was dead.

Natick Trolley

Onlookers on the trolley stared at him and moved to other seats to distance themselves from him and his deceased child.

When the trolley came to a stop, Giuseppe exited. He carried his lifeless daughter's body to a bench at the trolley stop and waited. It would be nearly an hour before another warm trolley arrived to take them back to Natick.

No one offered him help for fear of getting sick. At that time the flu epidemic (called the Spanish Flu) was in full force. It had been killing people since 1918, and more than fifty million people would die before it ended.

Giuseppe and Vincenza buried Christina in the yard at the Rossi residence and planted a small oak tree beside her grave. The immediate family, the Berons, and Father Tirrochi from Sacred Heart Church attended her burial.

The devastated couple would mourn the tragic loss of their child for the rest of their lives. Fortunately, their family would continue to grow again in the near future.

Note: I attempted to locate Christina's birth and death records while I was in the Vital Records department of the Warwick Town Hall. No records could be located, though it is quite possible that I did not have the correct date of her passing. The attending clerk suggested that Christina might have been born at home as well as buried at home, which was not uncommon during that time period. The fact that she even existed came from my conversation with Uncle Nick, who had been a child himself when Christina passed.

An Internet search on Roots Web and Ancestry.com, as well as the Rhode Island census, also yielded no results. I could not locate any record indicating the existence of Christina Rossi, and that bothered me.

One night while sleeping, I awoke, as I often do, with an immediate need to use the restroom. As I rolled over and opened my eyes to get off the bed, I realized that there was a purple haze in the room. I tried to focus my eyes, but the haze remained the same. The room was dark but had enough light for me to see where I needed to go.

As I walked toward the archway leading to the master bathroom, behind one of the bedroom's entry double doors stood the spirit of a young girl.

I immediately got chills from head to toe as our eyes met. I knew who she was, but I could not believe my eyes. Was I dreaming?

She was wearing a white dress; her dark hair was neatly curled in the 1920s fashion. She was less than four feet tall and had a round face with rosy red cheeks. There was a glow about her presence.

She smiled at me as I passed. Her head was tilted downward; her eyes looked upward. I showed no emotion and kept walking, partly out of fear and disbelief and partly out of embarrassment, as I was only dressed only in my underwear.

I returned to the room moments later with a sense that I had nothing to fear— the purple haze was gone; Christina was gone.

I quickly realized that she had come to let me know that she had in fact existed.

To my own surprise, I went back to bed and slept contently.

Thank you, Christina, for your visit!

28 THE REVOLVING DOOR

In September of 1920, Giuseppe—determined to sell his weapon—changed his stained work shirt for a crisp white one and left work at eleven thirty in the morning from the Providence-based American Screw Company and proceeded to the Rhode Island state capitol building. A set of flying torpedo drawings in hand, he had firm plans to speak with Governor R. Livingston Beeckman about his invention. Perhaps the man who held the highest office in the state could help him sell his invention to Washington.

"I would like to speak with the governor please," he requested of the receptionist.

"May I ask your name please, sir?" she asked politely.

"Giuseppe Rossi."

"Do you have an appointment to see the governor, Mr. Rossi?"

"No, but I can assure you that I won't take much of his time. I simply want to show him some drawings," Giuseppe responded quickly.

"May I ask what the drawings are in reference to, Mr. Rossi?" she asked.

"A military device," he said patiently.

Rhode Island Governor 1915 to 1921
R. Livingston Beeckman

114

"I can try to get you in, sir, but it is twelve o'clock, sir. The governor takes his lunch from twelve to one. You are welcome to wait here," she said, pointing to a set of red leather chairs.

At one p.m. sharp, Giuseppe inquired at the reception desk if he could meet with the governor; he was declined.

He received the same response at two, three, and again at four.

"We are very sorry, sir, but the governor simply refuses to meet with you without an appointment. *You must have an appointment*," the receptionist said in an annoyed tone with her index finger pointing at him.

"Would you like to make an appointment?" she asked.

Tired, hungry, frustrated, and now angry, Giuseppe responded in a low tone of voice. *"Please tell the governor I have two words for him, and they are not Merry Christmas!"*

As Giuseppe departed down the front steps of the capitol, he looked backed toward the building; in one of the windows, holding back a curtain, was the governor staring at him.

In what appeared to be a sudden burst of laughter, the governor released his hold on the curtain and disappeared from sight.

Angry and disappointed, Giuseppe looked for the closest place to get a drink to calm his nerves before making his way home.

Rhode Island State Capitol

Standing outside of the Biltmore Hotel, he encountered something he had never seen before—a revolving glass door. He stepped up to the left side of the door but did not see a handle; he pushed on the door, but it did not budge. He looked to the right side and did not see a handle.

He stepped back from the revolving door to look for another entrance. Suddenly a woman carrying a drink emerged from the left side of the revolving door; again it closed.

Giuseppe returned to the left side of the revolving door and pushed; it would not budge. He could not pull the door; it had no handles.

Completely frustrated and totally impatient, he stepped back from the door, found a rock that was about six inches in diameter, looked around to see if anyone was watching him, and plunged it through the glass door. Giuseppe stepped over the broken glass and walked down the hotel hallway toward the bar as though he were a guest. A hotel porter who'd heard the crashing glass passed Giuseppe in the hallway.

"Some asshole just broke your glass door," he exclaimed to the porter. "Merry Christmas," he added.

With a grin from ear to ear, Giuseppe sat down at the bar and ordered himself a drink.

The Sheraton Biltmore Hotel

29 TURMOIL IN THE VILLAGE

A couple of years passed, and Giuseppe was just trying to make ends meet. On January 20, 1922, a small article in the local newspaper, *The Times*, ushered the state of Rhode Island into a thirty-three-week-long crisis. Hardship hit thousands of families, including the Rossis.

When the story was released, no one knew the extent of the devastation it would bring. The headline read, "Cut in Wages Announced for Valley Mills."

The story stated that some twenty-five thousand millworkers would be affected by a 20 to 22 percent wage cut in the mills of the Goddard Brothers and the B.B. & R. Knight Company. At the time, mill workers earned thirty dollars for a forty-eight-hour week. Additionally, mills in Riverpoint, Phoenix, Arctic, Centerville, and Hope would be affected by the cut.

Although Giuseppe worked in Providence, he also relied on the mills as a second income to support his family. He would often work nights and weekends repairing the looms and other machinery. Management often contacted him to fill in when their millwrights were absent.

Traveling by trolley to Providence became unsafe and nearly impossible as unemployed mill workers paralyzed the valley and would stop anyone who would attempt to go to work at the mills and cross picket lines.

Rioting erupted on January 31, 1922, at the Natick mill. The mob, completely out of control because of a rioter that had been arrested, smashed windows and threw stones at the mill. Men delivering goods by truck at the Arkwright mill loading docks in Coventry were beaten. Demonstrations turned violent, outbreaks of lawlessness and violence went unchecked, and by the end of it, people were hurt and killed.

When local police could not control the violence, Rhode Island Governor Emory J. San Souci activated the Pawtucket Armory National Guard on February 20, 1922.

Rhode Island National Guardsmen on the Rooftop of the Natick Mill

Armory, Pawtucket, Rhode Island

Rhode Island Governor Emery J. San Souci
1921–1923

Guardsman set up a machine gun on top of the Natick Mill to prevent a possible attack on the mill, which had already been the scene of a number of bloody fights and riots. The residents of Natick feared that martial law might come to their town. Those who lived in company housing were threatened with eviction.

When the strike ended, families struggled to regain their normal lives, and many small businesses had closed. Large businesses suffered great revenue losses with lost clients and goods. Ultimately, many folks still lost their jobs, and the area suffered.

Fortunately, Giuseppe's mechanical skills were now in great demand at the mills, and his daily commute trolleys were back in service. In addition, Giuseppe still worked hard to have his homemade aerial torpedo sold. And true to his word, Ordinance Officer Meriden sent weapons contractors to Giuseppe's doorstep regularly. Throughout the remainder of the 1920s men in suits visited the Rossi residence to view the flying torpedo—they came, they saw, but no sale.

30 THE CROMPTON LIBRARY

With only two days remaining of my visit to Rhode Island, I contemplated how best to spend the rest of the time. I was still in disbelief of my findings at the Warwick Town Hall, but nothing short of body exhumations and autopsy would satisfy my suspicions. I guess I watched too many forensic television shows to believe the coroner death certificate findings; it was unsettling.

I was sitting at Mom's kitchen table having coffee when she handed me a newspaper clipping, a photo of her father that had appeared in the local paper. Beneath the photo the small type stated that the picture came from "The Pawtuxet Valley Preservation and Historical Society." I had passed this place several times during my visit. The building was the old Crompton Library I remembered and had visited as a child, not far from Mom's house on Main Street.

Mom and I decided to pay them a visit.

It was a trip back in time for me to walk into the old library building, which had been built in 1876. The walls and old wooden floors had not changed. Yet the library books and bookshelves that I remembered had been replaced with newer shelves of donated books, photographs, and memorabilia. There were artifacts relating to life in Pawtuxet Valley, including textile manufacturing, military, fire, police, and sports objects. We showed the volunteer curator the newspaper clipping of my mother's father, and he descended to the basement where the actual photo was stored in a metal file cabinet, leaving myself, Mom, and one other man to browse the main floor. As I viewed the secured glass cases of military photos, ribbons, medals, helmets, leather gun belts, and boots that had been acquired mostly by donation, I was thinking out loud when I suggested to Mom that it would be great if I could learn more about the army ordinance officer who had helped my grandfather Giuseppe. I am not sure she knew what I was talking about—she had a distant look on her face—but she nodded and agreed.

The curator soon returned and said he had located the photo and that he could not offer me the original photo but could scan the picture and place it on a disk. He also asked if he could help with anything else.

After seeing some of the textile photos on display, I asked for copies; I hated to impose on the curator, but I had to take advantage of the moment. I offered to pay for this service, and he refused but did suggest that a donation to the preservation society would be appreciated.

The obliging curator agreed to help me and again descended to the basement. I assumed that the elderly person who was still browsing the main floor with Mom and me was affiliated with the museum, but I soon learned he was not.

As our paths inevitably crossed within the narrow aisles of the small building, I asked the gentleman, out of sheer curiosity, "Are you a curator here, sir?"

"Oh no," he said. "I simply like to visit this place for a few minutes once or twice a week to see what's new. It's not far from my home," he explained with a big smile.

"My name is Serifino Orso. My friends call me 'Fino.' Who might you be?" His hand extended for a handshake.

"I'm Richard Rossi." As we shook hands, I realized that this senior citizen had the iron grip of an athlete. "And this is my mom, Rita Rossi."

"It's always nice to meet some new faces in this old building," Serifino said as he faced my mother.

"Thank you, Mr. Orso," Mom replied. "It is a pleasure to meet you also."

"Please, call me Fino. Mr. Orso was my father," he said as he shook hands with Mom. "This building is so very small and sound travels easily," Serifino said apologetically. "I wasn't eavesdropping, but I heard you ask your mom about a military officer. May I ask who he was? Perhaps I can help."

Just then, the curator returned with a CD disk in a paper CD envelope. "Here are the pictures you requested. Can we offer any further assistance to you today?" he asked.

Serifino interrupted before I could answer. "I have an unofficial database of military persons from the surrounding cities. Perhaps we can find the person you are looking for."

"He doesn't offer that opportunity to many people, especially strangers," the curator said laughingly. "I've seen his collection. If you are looking for someone in particular, you would be wise to take a quick look," he continued as he nodded his head with a motion that I should be nodding yes to Serifino's offer.

"You are welcome to come and view the records as well, Mrs. Rossi," said Serifino. Mom politely declined; she was more concerned about getting dinner started.

I answered without a second thought. "Very well, Fino. Thank you for your offer. I would appreciate your help."

After dropping Mom off at her house, I proceeded to the address that Serifino had provided using my GPS. His home really was a few short blocks from the museum.

As I pulled into Serifino's driveway, I noticed that it was the most meticulously kept home on the block. It was beginning to get late; the sun was setting. My mom was preparing a special dinner for my daughter and me, and we still needed to get our belongings organized for our early-morning departure, so I felt a bit rushed—yet I was anxious to find out if Fino could actually find information for me on the ordinance officer who had been in close contact with my grandfather.

"You must be Mr. Rossi," the woman who answered the door said. "I'm Fino's wife Zita. Please come in."

"I'm pleased to meet you, Zita," I said as we walked up a few stairs leading to the main floor of the raised ranch.

"Serifino's in his office. SERIFINO, SERIFINO," Zita yelled down the hallway to her husband.

"He doesn't hear well these days," she said with a smile. "Walk to the end of the hall, he's in the office. I must apologize—I'm busy in the kitchen. Please excuse me," she said as she slipped her apron over her head. "Italian cookies," she said with a grin. "Family recipe." I was salivating over the aroma of anisette.

As I entered the room at the end of the hallway, my eyes opened wide; the walls were covered pictures of military folks, including a great photo of Serifino with his father *and* son in uniform.

Serifino could see that I was in a state of amazement as he got up from his black leather chair to shake hands with me.

"After I enlisted into the army in 1943, my bride Zita began saving newspaper articles of local soldier stories and war-related events from several different newspapers. The idea was that when I got home, I could see what had happened to other soldiers from the area. As it turned out, some of my classmates from school—friends actually—never made it home. Some were decorated for bravery in battle."

It was obvious that Serifino was saddened by the loss of his childhood schoolmates; I could hear it in his voice.

"Zita and I decided to continue to do this after I got home in '45. It was our way of showing respect to those who put themselves in harm's way."

Not knowing exactly what information Serifino and Zita had compiled, I was not sure how Serifino intended to help me.

"Let's see. Was your dad in the military?"

"Yes," I said.

"Name," he asked.

"Gennaro Rossi," I said.

"Two *n*'s in Gennaro?"

"Yes."

"Serifino, dinner's almost ready," Zita yelled from the kitchen.

"I won't keep you, Serifino—" I began to say.

"Here. 'BATTLE STARS ARE RECEIVED Pfc. Gennaro J. Rossi of Natick for His Service Abroad.' Is that him?"

"Yes! Holy smokes! I cannot believe it! That's amazing!"

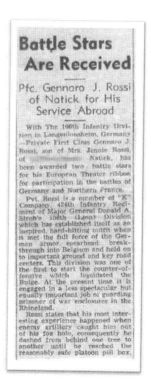

Battle Stars Are Received

Pfc. Gennaro J. Rossi of Natick for His Service Abroad

With The 100th Infantry Division in Langenlonsheim, Germany Private First Class Gennaro J. Rossi, son of Mrs. Jennie Rossi, of _____ Natick, has been awarded two battle stars for his European Theater ribbon for participation in the battles of Germany and Northern France.

Pvt. Rossi is a member of "K" Company, 424th Infantry Regiment of Major General Donald A. Stroh's 106th (Lion) Division which has established itself as an inspired, hard-hitting outfit when it met the full force of the German armor spearhead breakthrough into Belgium and held on to important ground and key road centers. This division was one of the first to start the counter-offensive which liquidated the Bulge. At the present time, it is engaged in a less spectacular but equally important job of guarding prisoner of war enclosures in the Rhineland.

Rossi states that his most interesting experience happened when enemy artillery caught him out of his fox hole, consequently he dashed from behind one tree to another until he reached the reasonably safe platoon pill box.

Serifino printed the article for me. Zita entered the room with a paper plate filled with Italian cookie delights covered with clear plastic wrap and a ribbon bow.

"Please take these to your mother's house. I've made extra...enjoy!" she said.

By now, I was beginning to feel as though I was imposing. It was their dinnertime, but I did not really want to leave. Serifino's database may have held some answers for me.

"Wow, you folks are great. Thank you so much," I said bowing as I took the dish full of confectionary treats. "I really should be going so you can eat your dinner, and I'm guessing it is about dinnertime at my mother's house as well."

"Can you come back in the morning, say nine o'clock?" Serifino asked.

Thinking quickly, I responded, "Yes, but only for a short time. I've got to catch a flight back to California."

"Before you leave, tell me who or what are you looking for. What is it that you...don't know?" Serifino asked.

"My grandfather worked with an army ordinance officer around the years of 1916 to 1919. I don't know his name," I said.

"Okay, my database does not include those years, but I will check anyway," Serifino said. "Any other information you can give me that might be helpful when I search?" he asked as he made notes on a yellow-lined pad of paper that he had on his desk.

"Yes, something I have not been able to figure out—the numbers 021646 and the letters RMII."

"Anything else?" he asked.

"My brother served in Vietnam."

"Full name?" he asked.

"Jerry Rossi."

"Okay. Not a lot to go on, but we'll see what we can find. I will see you in the morning," he said as he continued to scribble down my request.

I returned to mom's house where dinner had been ready for over an hour, although Alecia and my mother had waited for me. I handed the copy of the newspaper clipping to my mother.

"What's this?" she asked as she took the paper from me. As she read the headlines, she held the paper to her chest; her eyes welled up with tears. However, without missing a beat, she pulled a chair out for me and told me to sit. "Your dinner's getting cold," she said.

She had made my favorite dish, stuffed cabbage rolls—golumpkies!

She placed the newspaper article in her bedroom on the nightstand beside the bed.

After dinner, Alecia contacted Southwest Airlines and easily rescheduled our departure time for around noontime the next day. Then we helped clear the dinner table, and my mom started washing dishes in the pantry.

"Was Serifino able to help you?" she inquired.

"Gosh, I don't know yet. That's why I'm going back to his house in the morning.

"I asked him to find Jerry Rossi since he found the article about Dad. I was curious to see if he had anything about Jerry."

"What's that got to do with your grandfather? Isn't this about him?" she asked.

"Yes, it is. But I didn't have much for him to go on. I gave him some numbers that I don't know the meaning of."

"Numbers? What numbers?" she asked intently.

"The numbers 021646," I replied. I had not mentioned these numbers to her before, and my mom looked at me with that blank stare that I had seen earlier at the museum. Her eyebrows went up; her mouth dropped open slightly.

"What is it, Mom? You had that look on your face earlier today. What are you thinking?"

"It has nothing to do with your grandfather because he was long, long gone at the time, but *your* father and I got married on February 16, 1946."

Interesting, I thought, but it really was a long time after my grandfather had passed away.

"I also gave Serifino the letters RMII, but I can't imagine what he will do with them," I said.

Again, I noticed Mom get a distant look on her face.

"Ma?" I asked.

"It's nothing...really," she said as she walked into the pantry and began washing the dinner dishes.

World War II Arial Torpedo "Buzz Bomb"
Damaged Buildings and Village

31 THE GREAT DEPRESSION

The year 1929 brought more despair to the Rossi household—the beginning of the Great Depression.

Although Giuseppe and Vincenza had saved some money for family emergencies, nothing, including the strike of 1922, could have prepared them for the coming of the worldwide economic devastation that would last through the late 1930s.

Having a large family meant being frugal to survive was a way of life for the Rossi family. Giuseppe was fortunate to have full-time work available in Providence and part-time work locally in Natick; however, it was often difficult to commute to Providence. Either there was no gasoline available for purchase or no funds to make the purchase. Likewise, public transportation was often not available; it became a luxury to ride the train or trolley.

The onset of the winter months brought additional transportation difficulties to contend with—vehicles that would not start and long commute times due to treacherous unplowed icy road conditions. On several occasions Giuseppe's car failed to start. Having worked a double shift, he sometimes would not make the trek home. Instead he would volunteer for the night shift as boiler watchman and then secretly sleep in the chair at the desk in the boiler room of the mill where it was toasty warm. The rumbling of the coal-fired boiler would lull him to sleep. It was music to his ears.

Like a good watchdog, though, when any unusual noise occurred, he would wake immediately and investigate. But fortunately, things usually ran quite smoothly.

32 THE ORDINANCE OFFICER

I arrived at the Orso home promptly at 9:00 a.m. as requested. Serifino met me at the front door, and Zita had a fresh pot of coffee brewing. The aroma was overwhelmingly inviting.

Serifino offered me a cup as he poured himself one, and I gladly accepted. "With cream please," I requested.

"Serifino, I won't be disappointed if you tell me you couldn't find any information with the small amount of info I supplied you, but did you have any luck?"

"Actually, I didn't research it at all. Zita is the computer expert in this house. I asked her to do it. It's her baby, and I believe she may have something of interest for you," he said hesitantly.

I am sure my facial expression changed when I heard those words. My heart began to beat a little faster. *Could Zita have some new clue for me?*

"Serifino..." Zita's voice trailed from the computer room down the hallway. "Have Richard come here please!" she yelled. "And give Richard some cookies to go with his coffee," she shouted.

I did not want to be rude to their hospitality, so I immediately grabbed a napkin-full of homemade Italian cookies from the platter on the counter and bolted down the hall where Zita was sitting at the computer.

"Good morning, Zita! Your coffee and cookies are amazing," I said as I entered the room.

"Thank you," she said. "Come sit beside me so I can show you what I've found." She tapped on a metal folding chair she had placed next to her. I sat quickly, trying to hang onto my remaining cookies and coffee. I could hear excitement in Zita's voice.

"I have several ways to research the data we have compiled over the years—by date, by name, or by an event. I started my search with the numbers you left with Serifino, 021646. I thought perhaps it was a date.

Unfortunately it turned up nothing tangible, so I pulled up an alphabetical list of names we have assembled and attempted to match the RMII, assuming that they were someone's initials. Here's what I found."

Zita pulled up a newspaper article dated February 1956; the headline read, "Soldier's Death Still a Complete Mystery."

The story was an interview with Robert Meriden II regarding the suspicious death of his father, retired army officer Robert Meriden Sr. The incident had taken place ten years earlier on the morning of February 16, 1946, in the Natick section of Warwick.

According to the article, the elder Meriden was found slumped over in his fishing boat floating in the Pawtuxet River with a bullet hole in his forehead. Police investigators at that time ruled the death a suicide; however, no weapon was ever found. His son, Robert Meriden II, believed that his father was murdered, yet he had no proof. "My father had no reason to kill himself," he proclaimed.

Robert Meriden Sr.'s military career spanned from 1916 to 1936; some of his earlier duties included ordinance officer based in the city of Providence War Department, and he was promoted to greater responsibility positions during the course his career.

Robert Meriden II was also a career military man, having worked at the Department of Defense in Washington, DC, for the latter part of his career. Meriden Jr. had requested that local police reopen the case involving his father's death; however, they declined, stating "insufficient evidence."

The interview had been conducted at Meriden's residence in Warwick—the house that had once belonged to Robert Meriden Sr. The article provided an exact address and photo of the younger Meriden standing in front of his late father's former home.

"Zita, this is amazing. You have solved my riddle with virtually no clues! Simply outstanding. Thank you so much!"

"You're welcome. I am glad we were a help to you, but we are not finished. Here is an article about your brother, Jerry," she said with a beaming smile and handed me copies of the articles.

Pfc. Jerry T. Rossi

Soldier From West Warwick Receives Medal

Pfc. Jerry T. Rossi of West Warwick, recently was awarded the Army Commendation Medal with the "V" device for heroism in Vietnam on Sept. 9. As a member of a reconnaissance patrol in the Phuoc Thanh Province, he crawled forward under heavy fire and obtained secure positioning for his squad's left flank.

Still not contented with his position, he rose and ran forward to a position squarely on the enemy's flank. From there he began a deadly volume of fire on the insurgent position, according to the citation.

Somewhat blown away, I again thanked Zita and Serifino, and I exited the Orso residence. I immediately phoned my daughter, Alecia, on the cell and let her know I would be returning to my mother's house in a matter of minutes. We had loaded our luggage into the trunk of the rental car the night before. Our motivation was to lessen the impact of leaving Mom's house and prevent her from seeing us carrying luggage. Saying good-bye was always difficult—especially since we never knew when we would fly back.

"How did that go?" my mom asked as I entered her house.

"You're not going to believe this, but Mrs. Orso may have actually found my missing ordinance officer, *and* there is possibility that his son may be living in Warwick," I said.

"I grew up in Warwick," Mom said. "It was a small town then. What is their name?" she asked.

"Meriden…Robert Meriden Sr. was the ordinance officer. His son is Robert Meriden the Second," I said as I handed her the copy of the newspaper clipping.

"Apparently Senior committed suicide on February 16, 1946, and the son thought he was murdered," I added.

Mom put her reading glasses on and sat down at the kitchen table to look over the article.

"February 16, 1946…that's the day your father and I got married, but I don't remember ever hearing about this," she said as though she was straining to remember.

Alecia glanced in my direction and gave me "the look"; it was time to hit the road.

Suddenly, Mom looked up from the article and got that—now familiar—faraway look in her eyes.

"Are you okay, Mom?" I asked. "What is it? Do you feel okay?" Mom suddenly looked a bit pale, and I became concerned.

"This happened right near where I grew up on East Avenue. I know who these people are," she said quietly.

"Bobby Meriden would come with his father to my dad's ice cream shop in Natick. He would play with us kids in the lot behind the store. The men would smoke cigars and talk while we kids played with my brothers and sisters," she said.

"I didn't know his father. He looked mean, but I was just a kid. I often wondered what happened to Bobby because he and his dad suddenly stopped coming to the store."

"That's incredible, Mom. Talk about a small world. Do you think Bobby Meriden could still be alive?" I asked.

"It's possible, I suppose. He was my age or a little older, and, heck, I'm still kicking," she said laughingly.

33 MOURNING IN NATICK

The state of the economy seemed to be getting somewhat better as spring of 1935 rolled around. Giuseppe and Vincenza were able to salt away a handful of dollars for the first time in many years. It was not much, but it let them feel somewhat financially secure.

Giuseppe still worked as hard, but for the first time in a long time, he felt good about himself and his family's future. Occasionally he would honor the day of rest and stay home from work to be with his family and friends.

Tragically, on May 28, 1935, Henry Beron's wife, Rosilda, suddenly passed after a two-day illness with pneumonia. She was only fifty years old. Rosilda's passing was devastating to Henry and his children as she was an integral part of all their lives. The entire hamlet of Natick mourned her passing—anyone who frequented the Beron's ice cream store knew the kind, gentle person she was.

Giuseppe and Vincenza were equally devastated.

The Beron family was more than just close friends—they were more like family. The Rossi family helped Henry and his children with the funeral arrangements. Giuseppe hoped to do more for his friend but could not afford to do so.

The Beron Family
Rosilda, Florence, Henry, Lawrence
Edmond, Rita, Bertha, Delia

Rosilda Beron

Mrs. Rosilda Beron is Dead at Natick; Funeral on Friday

Mrs. Rosilda Beron, wife of Henry Beron, died this morning at her home, 2 East avenue, Natick, in her 50th year, following a short illness with pneumonia. She was born in Natick, November 4, 1885, a daughter of the late Joseph and Rosilda (Monjeau) Duminie.

Besides her husband she leaves two sons, Lawrence and Edmond Beron; four daughters, Florence, Delia, Bertha and Rita Beron; two brothers, Walter and Albert Duminie; two sisters, Mrs. Desiree Sauliere of Natick and Mrs. Raoul Danjou of Providence. She was a member of the Sodality of St. Anne.

The body, which was removed to the Thomas Robert & Son Funeral parlors, will be taken to her home late this afternoon. The funeral will be held there Friday morning, at 8:15, followed by Requiem Mass at St. Joseph's Church, Natick, at 9 o'clock.

Sadly, Rosilda had passed away only two days after Rita Beron's eleventh birthday. During the funeral reception, Rita could no longer hold back her emotions and ran out of the Thomas Robert & Son funeral parlor where she cried profusely as she sat on a wooden bench.

Gennaro Rossi (about the same age as Rita) was standing outside the funeral home. He tried to console Rita, but she was extremely upset.

One of Gennaro's older brothers peered out the double front entrance doors of the funeral home to see where Gennaro was. He could not see that it was Rita who was on the bench.

"Jerry, get in here and stop playing with that girl," he yelled.

Gennaro stayed and talked with Rita until she stopped crying.

34 MERIDEN S HOUSE

Just as we were leaving my mom's house, Alecia received a notification text on her cell phone from the airline that our flight would be delayed thirty minutes. We were already quite early, but we needed to fill the gas tank and return the rental car to an off-site location.

"I Google-mapped Meriden's home address," Alecia said. "It's not far from the airport. Some place called Governor Francis Estates. Do you want to swing by there to see the place? I can punch it into the GPS."

Looking over the top of my glasses I responded with an emphatic "Yes!" as I pushed down a bit harder onto the car accelerator pedal.

35 COPIES TO ITALY AND GERMANY

Giuseppe knew that the life of his flying torpedo's seventeen-year patent was about to expire in a few weeks on June 24, 1936. Giuseppe did not receive a positive response from the US government to continue the patent or utilize the device, so he decided to branch out. He was motivated to make one last attempt to sell his invention—regardless of who the buyer might be. Not only was he proud of his work, he needed the money.

Maria offered to help her father. She prepared two neatly typed letters of introduction on a new Royal typewriter, which she'd borrowed from work. Each letter offered to sell patent rights and torpedo construction assistance for the device. The letters were neatly packaged with copies of the original patent drawings of the flying torpedo.

After exploring options of where to send the letter and patent, the first package was addressed to Italy. Maria boldly directed the offer for a flying torpedo to "His Excellency Benito Mussolini Head of Government."

The second package was addressed to Germany: *"Oberkommando des Heeres,"* the Supreme Command of the Army at the military operations command center. Both packages were mailed from the new post office in Pawtucket.

New Post Office, Pawtucket, Rhode Island

Two weeks after the document packages had been mailed to Europe, a chance meeting of Giuseppe and Robert Meriden occurred. A heated verbal discussion ensued after Giuseppe disclosed to Meriden the fact that he had sent torpedo plans and information out of the country.

Meriden became furious when Giuseppe blamed the failure to sell his prototype weapon on Meriden's poor sales skills and lack of aviation weaponry knowledge. And Rossi became infuriated when Meriden proclaimed that the device was inferior and simplistic, that it lacked a guidance system and therefore could not be used by the military or a private contractor.

What had once been a burgeoning friendship turned dramatically after the bitter dispute. The men parted ways huffing and puffing, each vowing to kick the other's ass when the opportunity presented itself.

US Army Officer Robert Meriden Sr. submitted a written "Unusual Occurrence" report of the incident to his superior officers—a move he would soon regret.

Benito Mussolini once boasted of
"secret weapons" to Adolph Hitler.

36 TWO-STORY GAMBREL

T here it is, Dad. That's the house. It hasn't changed a bit," Alecia said excitedly as we arrived, pointing at the house pictured in the newspaper article.

"Damn, you're right. It's like stepping back in time," I said, equally excited as I pulled up and parked directly across the street from the property. We sat in the car and admired the huge three-story gambrel-roofed house with blue and white trim and twin red brick chimneys. The shuttered windows complemented the beautiful ornately trimmed porch, which spanned the width of the front of the house. The landscaped plants had changed slightly, but the overall appearance of the home was the same as the newspaper photo Zita had printed for us from so many years ago.

On the left side of the house was the driveway, which consisted of a grass median bordered by two concrete strips that led to the rear of the house. At the end of the driveway was a two-story gambrel-roofed three-car garage. The second story of the garage had blinds in the windows that indicated it could possibly be a guest apartment.

As Alecia and I sat and admired the property, we soon realized that the three vehicles parked in front of the property actually belonged to contractors working on the house.

Pete's Greenscape, O'Donnell's Window and Door, and Work of Art Painters—all of which were busy working on the property.

"This is not a good sign, Lee."

"Why is that, Dad?" she asked.

"Men in their mid- to late-eighties don't spend the kind of money it takes to have all these contractors working on their house," I answered with a slight tone of disappointment.

"Dad, there's a man working on a motorcycle in the garage. Maybe you should go talk to him," Alecia suggested.

Just then, her cell phone rang. "It's Aaron," she said excitedly. "He's home from his European tour! He said he has one last huge show to play in Los Angeles and he wants all of us to be there!"

"Absolutely! Tell him we *will* be there. Tell him I said, 'Welcome home,' and that we love him.

"Okay, I am going to talk to the guy in the garage," I said as I took in a deep breath and began to get out of the car.

As I walked toward the garage, I expected the person in jeans and denim jacket with cutoff sleeves wearing dark shades to acknowledge my nearing approach. When he finally looked in my direction, he was not looking at me but past me toward the street where I had originated. I thought perhaps Alecia had decided to join me and was walking toward the garage. I glanced back and saw a black vehicle with limo-tint windows pull up behind my rental car. A disgruntled look suddenly appeared on the face of the individual I was now standing in front of.

"Whateva it is yaw' sellin'—I already got two, so you can leave. Take ya friends out in the street with ya," he said in a thick Rhode Island accent without even looking at me. He was using two fingers to point to the black car in the street, suggesting they were my "friends."

He then turned toward his wood workbench and turned up the volume on his beat-up garage stereo, which was playing some awful rockabilly music. The back of his jeans jacket had a silhouette of a combat soldier with "65-68" embroidered beneath it.

What an asshole. I have come a long way, and I want some answers, damn it.

He turned back toward his motorcycle, but I was still standing there.

"I'm sorry if I have disturbed you, sir. I was hoping to find Mr. Robert Meriden the Second living at this address. I'm not selling anything, and I do not know who is in the black car in the street," I said aggressively. "Go fuck yourself very much" was what I really wanted to say.

"Who-a' you? Whudda ya want Robert fo'?" he asked, as he reached for a cell phone on the workbench. He then seemingly punched in a text message, still not looking my direction.

"My name is Richard Rossi. Robert's father—Robert Meriden Sr.— helped my grandfather Giuseppe Rossi with getting a patent for his flying torpedo back in 1919. I was hoping to talk to him to see if he remembered anything or if his father left behind any records," I said in a calmer tone of voice, hoping to solicit some help from this guy.

After a brief moment of silence, a dropped jaw, and slightly pale white face, the man looked upward toward the ceiling and then in my direction, and was apparently at a loss for words.

"How'd you find the house?" he asked. I handed him the newspaper article that Zita had printed for me. He briefly glanced at it and handed it back to me. It was as if he had seen the article before.

"Robert died eight months ago. His greedy fuckin' gold-diggin' relatives including his money-suckin' nephew lawyer cleaned out the house of everything. They left the cellar and garage trash behind for me to clean up...those assholes!" he blurted. The vein in the center of his forehead was bulging.

I was staring at him, and now I was the one with the dropped jaw.

"Oh, hey man, I'm venting—sorry. I bought the estate for cheap because the rest of them didn't want to deal with it," he said. "I kinda grew up in this house.

"There are some ancient files in boxes right here." He pointed to boxes covered with plastic on the garage floor. "And some in the basement and upstairs." He pointed to the second level of the garage. "What is it you're looking for exactly?"

"Anything regarding my grandfather, Giuseppe Rossi, and his flying torpedo. My grandfather and his daughter died suspiciously on the same day in 1937. So I am trying to find out what happened to them and the torpedo."

"Hmmm, suspiciously? Aay...why dya say dat?" he asked.

"Sources tell me that neither one was sick before they died," I said.

Suddenly, two loud, highly customized choppers entered the driveway, one on each of the concrete strips. The noise was deafening as they sped toward the garage. The bikers mindlessly revved their engines several times before shutting them down. The duo was about the same age as the person in the garage, late fifties to early sixties, and wearing the same combat soldier silhouetted jackets and dark glasses. Both had gray hair ponytails; one had a goatee, the other a fu man chu.

The three men were now looking at me with a *'Why haven't you left yet?'* expression on their faces.

Humbly, I finally said, "I have taken enough of your time, sir. I have a plane to catch, thanks."

"Hey, leave me your contact information, in case I find something when I go through this stuff," the garage person said.

"Sure," I said. I took my personal business card from my wallet, wrote my home and email addresses on the back, and handed it to him.

"I didn't get your name, sir," I said with my hand extended to shake his hand.

"That's cause I didn't give it to ya," he said. The biker trio laughed as I exited the garage. Needless to say, there was no handshake.

Patiently waiting in the rental car, Alecia rolled down the driver's window and unlocked the doors as I crossed the road. She motioned to me with her eyes to look at the car parked behind us.

The vehicle was a Dodge Charger, black with black wheels, small chrome center hubcaps on some beefy wide tires. Two men with white shirts and ties sat inside—both staring at me as I walked to the car and began to get in. Taking one last glance behind me before I got in the rental, I noticed that behind the grill of the car were red and blue lights.

37 SOLDIER DISMISSED

Robert Meriden was only months away from being eligible for a twenty-year retirement from the military when his superiors summoned him to an inquiry. At the Providence Armory behind a closed door in a red mahogany-paneled room, Meriden was sharply dressed in full uniform. Patiently he waited for his superior officers to arrive and assumed the meeting was a "preretirement" discussion—that he would be congratulated for his career highlights and accomplishments. Four superior officers arrived, entering the room in solemn silence without acknowledging Meriden's presence. Meriden rose from his seat when the door opened, stood at attention, and saluted his superior officers. The four officers, now facing Meriden, saluted him.

"As you were, soldier. You may be seated," one of them barked.

The meeting started and concluded in less than thirty minutes. The four superior officers promptly left the room. Meriden stayed in the room, closed the door, and sat quietly by himself.

The panel of officers—two of whom had had conflict with Robert Meriden in the past—had reviewed the "Unusual Incident" report Meriden submitted regarding Giuseppe Rossi having sent his torpedo drawings to foreign countries, Germany and Italy.

Meriden was reprimanded for allowing a "breach of national security" to occur by a naturalized citizen—particularly one that he was directly responsible for overseeing concerning the construction of a prototype weapon of war. Had he submitted his report in a timelier manner, United States postal authorities may have prevented the torpedo drawing packages from being delivered to foreign military powers. Additionally, complaints had reportedly been filed with the Office of Military Affairs that Meriden acted in a manner unbecoming an officer of the United States Military, "often under the influence of alcohol" both "off duty" as well as "on duty in uniform."

Officer Meriden was summarily advised to immediately submit a Request for Retirement from military service if he wished to obtain an Honorable Discharge.

In the thirty-minute conference period, he was not allowed to speak one word in his own defense.

Falling short of the full twenty-year retirement time required, his reduced monthly retirement paycheck would be considerably less than anticipated. Meriden became angry and upset that his military career was in ruins. He promptly left the armory office and headed to a nearby bar, where he buried his sorrows in the bottom of a bottle.

Meriden would need to go home and explain to his family that he was being forced to retire early. This would be a hefty blow on family finances, and his wife, Emily (known as Emma to friends and family), would be devastated. As Robert drowned his issues in the bottle, so would Emma. Emma's addiction to alcohol transformed into chronic liver disease.

As Meriden coped with the loss of his career, his life continued to deconstruct. On Sunday, December 6, 1936, Robert's wife, Emma, passed away in her sleep. She was forty-nine years old.

38 PARANOIA STRIKES AGAIN

Getting back to reality in California, my daughter and I were overwhelmed with work that had accumulated at our places of employment. I was overbooked with service calls, but it was great to be home and wonderful to be needed. The weather was cool and dry, unlike the humidity and rain we'd experienced in Rhode Island.

Yes, I was back on freeways heavily burdened with traffic, but that was life in the Golden State. Really, I wouldn't trade it for anything.

It seemed like only two weeks after being back from Rhode Island that I once again had the uncomfortable feeling of being followed each time I left my home or work in my Ford F-150 pick-up.

Am I simply crazy with paranoia? Why would anyone want to follow me?

I overwhelmingly had this odd feeling that I was under surveillance. But why? By whom? I couldn't put my finger on it; it was simply this nagging gut feeling. The odd part was that the vehicles that I suspected were following me on the freeway appeared to be average everyday cars.

Notably, there was one person I felt like I was seeing repeatedly in a white van, one of those cubed-body delivery-type vehicles, not very big. The driver appeared to be in his late fifties to early sixties, clean-cut, wearing a uniform. There were no business signs on the truck. The truck was clean, almost new looking.

It was as if I had a chain tied to his bumper and I was towing him wherever I went, every turn I made. Each time I looked into my rearview mirror he was there, seemingly staring at me in my rearview mirror. Then suddenly he would turn off and was gone.

In another instance it was a gray high-performance Ford Mustang. Again, it seemed to be with me as I went from freeway to surface streets. This vehicle had plenty of opportunity and power to pass or overtake me at any time, but it always seemed to lurk behind me.

One early Sunday morning, Jan and I headed to San Clemente Pier for breakfast as we often did. Great view, good food, fresh ocean air. Yes, we were spoiled!

The restaurant door had just been unlocked as we entered with another early-bird couple. Seated outdoors on the wood-deck patio, we were over the water with waves crashing against the support pillars beneath us. The other couple was seated near us on the south end of the patio. The sun was rising behind us in the east; we had a clear view of the ocean and a gaggle of early morning surfers to watch as they tried to catch a wave. In a moment's time, a man dressed entirely in black clothing appeared in front of the other couple. He briefly spoke to them and then snapped their picture with a camera that was tethered around his neck.

Before I could put down the menu I was reading, he was standing in front of Jan and me, snapping our picture, without asking our permission or saying a word.

In an instant, he was gone. The whole thing was very strange and caught me off guard.

I did not think of myself as a paranoid person, so why did I keep feeling like I was under surveillance by deep undercover agents? Would there actually be an agency that would go to these lengths over a nobody like me? What had I done recently that would have triggered anyone to follow me? Maybe it *was* in my imagination.

Then it occurred to me. My thoughts reverted to my recent Rhode Island visit. Who had been in the black car that pulled up behind me at Robert Meriden the Second's house, and did it have anything to do with me? If so, what?

I was convinced I was being followed. I just had that feeling as the hairs on the back of my neck stood straight.

Later that week, an opportunity arose for Jan and me to attend a social gathering with some of her coworkers. We agreed it could not have come at a better time. Stephan and Rosemary would be there—and not only are they great people, but Stephan is a FBI agent.

During the party, Stephan was as bored as I was, and we easily struck up conversation. After trading niceties as to each other's families' health and well-being, I dove into the heart of the matter and began to tell him of my book writing and research escapades. This led up to my explanation of being followed and my paranoia syndrome. I explained the strange cars I had been seeing, the trip to Meriden's house in Rhode Island, and the type of web searches I had been conducting on early models of flying torpedoes and missiles.

"Stephan, maybe a lot of this is coincidence, but I keep getting this nagging feeling like I'm being followed. I keep wondering if I triggered some sort of government red flag or watch list or something. It's possible I'm just being paranoid. But I'm really glad you made it to this party tonight because I wanted to ask you if you can please check to see if I am on the FBI watch list."

Stephan laughed. "That's the first time anyone has *requested* me to investigate them. It's a bit unorthodox for me to initiate an investigation without a crime having been committed, but I can check our files to see if your name pops up."

I shook his hand and thanked him, and then we went back to being bored at the party.

Three days later, Stephan called and spoke with Jan. Apparently there were a number of "Richard Rossis" in the database, and he would need my Social Security number to narrow his search.

It would be another two weeks before I received information back from Stephan.

He called our home Thursday around 7:00 p.m. and left a message that simply said, "Richard, it's not us."

39 SOLDIER HITS ROCK BOTTOM

In the weeks following Emma's death, Robert Meriden made a conscious effort to get himself out of the downward spiraling state of depression that was consuming him. He was overwhelmingly distraught, alone, and feeling broken.

Robert Jr. had been home on military leave only long enough to attend the in-home wake and then bury his mom. He offered support to his dad, who had not had a drink of alcohol out of respect for his late wife. Robert Sr. was elated to see his son, regardless of the sad circumstances.

Neighborhood friends and a few of Emma's distant relatives attended the funeral (mostly out of curiosity) and kindly offered their condolences and support to Robert if he so needed. "All's you has to do is ask," they said in their Rhode Island manner of speech.

There were a number of things to tend to at the house since Emma's passing. Salvatore (Sal) Scullivino, the Meriden's next-door neighbor, offered to help Robert repair his car engine that had partially frozen, splitting the radiator cores wide open. Robert had failed to drain his engine block and radiator of cooling water the night he found his deceased wife in the house. At that time, only affluent people owned heated garages for their automobiles—and Meriden was not one of them. Robert accepted Sal's kind offer and was looking forward to getting at least one productive thing accomplished, knowing that working on the car would also be a good distraction. Without Emma, there was a huge void in his life, and his own house began to feel like a black hole.

Robert Meriden Sr. was dressed in a new black suit; he smiled, shook hands with his neighbors, accepted condolences politely, and was the perfect host to the attendees of his wife's funeral proceedings. Robert could not care less what most of these folks had to offer him. After all, he had rarely been home and did not personally know most of them. He *was* grateful that they attended for Emma's sake, but that was all. He believed that Emma was looking down from heaven, watching the proceedings, and would have been content.

Later that evening, mortuary personnel arrived to remove the casket from the home and took it to the mortuary to complete the funeral service the following morning. Meriden lost his composure as the men took his wife's body from their home.

Grief-stricken, Robert retreated to his bedroom and closed the door. Filled with emotion and regrets that he could have been a better husband to his beloved Emma, he cried himself to sleep.

The following morning after a brief ceremony at the gravesite, Robert Jr., who had not displayed any emotion up until this time, was visibly shaken. His father was not sure how to console him, as he himself was too overwhelmed with grief.

Midday the day of the funeral, Robert Sr. took a taxi ride with his son to the train station and watched him depart on the noon train back to his base for active duty. He was grateful to have been able to spend even a short time with his son.

Although he was a career-hardened military man, Robert Sr. found this to be one the most difficult periods in his entire life. Bury his devoted wife in the morning, and then ship his son back to the military where he would assuredly be placed into harm's way. The one day felt like a year, and Meriden was exhausted. He could hardly find the energy to get out of bed over the next week.

But Robert Sr. knew he had to get himself together. He needed a new source of income and a greater distraction from his empty house. He soon found full-time work at a lumberyard located on Post Road in Warwick. He felt surprisingly well being around people, helping them with hardware needs or selecting and loading lumber materials into their vehicles.

His life seemed to be finding some sort of new balance, until the week before Christmas. The lumberyard had just received a truckload of fresh-cut Christmas trees. Meriden Sr. assisted families and couples in selecting and loading their ideal Christmas trees. And at the end of the day, he went home to an empty house—no tree, no ornaments, no presents. It became emotionally draining; he was alone. No one to share dinner with, no one to talk to, and most overwhelming, no one to hold.

The day before Christmas, before it was even noon, Robert Sr. began making the rounds at his favorite watering holes in Providence: Hoyle Sq. Bar, then Imperial Café, and finally Maxie's Bar on Academy Avenue.

He had a grand time for himself; he saw his old drinking buddies and laughed about the good ole days. Even the bartenders in these establishments recognized him and were glad to see him. He was, after all, a good customer, a heavy drinker, and one who rarely caused any trouble.

Meriden missed the excitement this atmosphere had to offer. He felt alive there. More importantly, he was not sitting home—alone—feeling sorry for himself.

On Friday, December 25, 1936, he awoke Christmas morning in a strange place, in a strange bed, hungover, his stomach upset; he was alone and generally feeling like shit. He could not remember how he'd gotten to this place. Still fully dressed, he stunk profusely of cigarette smoke and spilled alcohol. Bleary-eyed, he read a small sign on the back of the hotel door that said City Hotel, Weybosset Street, Providence.

"How the fuck did I get here?" he whispered to himself, glancing back at the bed that looked like it had been trampled upon.

Robert sat on the small, flowery, tattered cloth-covered bench seat that he pulled out from under the mirrored oak vanity in the room and stared at himself in the mirror pondering his miserable self-worth. Suddenly, a feeling of complete and utter despair overcame him. He had once been a proud officer in the United States Army; now he saw himself as a lowly, drunken, depressed recluse of a man. Moreover, he was now staring at that man in the mirror.

"How the fuck did you get here, Robert?" he yelled loudly into the mirror. "How the fuck did you get here?"

Although still not completely sober, his random thoughts became clear to him. Self-pity soon became enraged anger. He reasoned that *he* had not brought this state of being upon himself—*other people* were responsible for his demise. *Other people* were responsible for ending his military career. *Other people* were responsible for him being a miserable drunkard.

He sat staring at himself in the mirror and continued to deconstruct his life. The reason *his* military career had met its early demise, the reason *he* had become depressed and suicidal, the reason *he* was on the bottom rung of life's ladder—the reason was actually *not* because of others.

No.

He had an epiphany.

It was because of one man!

Sadness, depression, self-pity, and anger suddenly disappeared from the reflected face in the mirror. It was replaced with a red-faced smile.

Lightning had struck, the light bulb had gone off—he'd figured it all out. Now standing, Robert Meriden pointed his finger at the reflection in the mirror and swore revenge for his miserable life on ONE individual.

"You will pay for this, fucker." He was still talking to the mirror with such conviction and only one person in mind. *"You will—"*

Just then, a door adjacent to the end of the bed swung open into the room from what appeared in the dim light to be a bathroom. Standing there in the doorway was a large figure of a busty woman smoking a cigarette. Robert immediately stood up, startled and somewhat bewildered. The woman reached to her left and pushed a wall switch button that controlled a small lamp with a yellowed lampshade on top of the dresser.

Robert recognized the woman known as Therese Skunk, a prostitute he'd met at one of his watering holes.

"Hi, Rob, honey, what's all the yelling about in here?" she asked. "Are you ready for round two, baby, or was last night enough for ya?"

40 CHRISTMAS 1936

Christmas holiday began Thursday, December 24, for the Rossi household. Vincenza was busy preparing a traditional Italian *Menu di Natale* (Christmas menu), including *pasta al forno* (baked pasta), and *cenci* (fried pastry ribbons sprinkled with powdered sugar). Maria Angelina stopped by with a platter of fresh-baked delights and wrapped gifts for the family. Giuseppe had worked a half-day at the textile mill and was now in the basement trying to decide which bottle of his homemade wine would be best with the pasta dinner.

The boys were outside, busy being boys. Playing catch and taking turns riding Nicholas's bicycle that he hated to share but accepted because there was only one bicycle in the household.

Midmorning on Christmas Eve, Henry Beron and his brother Alexis arrived at the Rossi front door unexpectedly bearing gifts. Henry presented Giuseppe with a box of imported cigars; Vincenza received a poinsettia plant to display on the front doorstep. The welcomed visitors sat in the warm kitchen briefly for a freshly made, hot cup of coffee, some colorful conversation, and some of Maria's delightful baked goods. It was a good day with family and friends, and everyone ate heartily.

Christmas morning Giuseppe awoke early, made his way downstairs to the kitchen, and heated some of yesterday's leftover coffee. He then planted himself in the living room where the Christmas tree stood with a bounty of gifts neatly wrapped at its base and stood guard. His youngest sons showed up first, yawning, rubbing their eyes, and in need of using the bathroom (which was outside in the cold). Eager to open their presents, they soon were dismayed by their dad's early Christmas morning request.

"I would like all of you to get dressed, have some breakfast, and be ready to go to early mass, as soon as possible. You can open your presents after we visit our good friend Reverend Tirrochi…and be sure to brush your teeth!" Giuseppe said with a raised voice, smiling, as the reluctant Rossi boys ran back to their rooms to get dressed.

At the Sacred Heart Church, Father Tirrochi delivered a joyous Christmas-spirited sermon to his parishioners who were dressed in their finest Christmas Day attire. He ended the prayers by saying, "May the Lord be with you, go in peace."

"Amen," replied the eager-to-leave parishioners.

Father Tirrochi quickly added, "Before you all leave for your Christmas Day celebration, may I ask the Rossi boys to stay behind and help me with a small task with tables and chairs in the Rectory Hall. I would like to invite everyone here this morning to join us for hot drinks and homemade treats in the Rectory Hall. All compliments of the Sacred Heart Church Activities Organization."

Sam and Tony noticed that Father Tirrochi made eye contact with Giuseppe and winked. The boys looked at each other with their mouths open; they knew they had been set up for something unpleasant.

"What are you up to, Papa?" asked Sam.

"Why do *we* have to stay behind?" asked Tony.

"Sorry, boys! Father Tirrochi needs your help setting up tables for this gathering. It will only take a few minutes." He was grinning. "I will see all of you at home afterwards," said Giuseppe to his boys.

"But Papa, we don't want to walk home. It's so cold outside," retorted Jerry. Sam, Tony, and Jerry looked at each other. They knew their dad was up to something, but they did not know what that *something* might be.

"See you at home, boys," said Giuseppe as he walked down the church steps.

One hour later, Nicholas, Samuel, Anthony, Lawrence, Michael, Gennaro, and Augustino arrived at home escorting their mother who had helped pass out hot drinks and goodies to the churchgoers. All were freezing from the cold.

Taking off their winter hats and coats, shrugging off the coldness from their bodies, they entered the small living room where their dad was on the floor playing with a small puppy.

Young Tony screamed, "Papa, got us a puppy!"

"Papa, is it a boy puppy or a girl puppy?" asked Larry.

"Does it have a name, Papa?" asked Jerry.

"It's a boy, and he does not have a name," answered Giuseppe, laughing. "You need to name him," he told his sons.

Gus bent down to pick the puppy up from the floor. The excited little puppy, which had not gone outside into the cold to do his business, suddenly squirted a stream of pee onto Gus's only Sunday "go to church" white shirt.

"AAAAH!" screamed Gus as he laughed.

"Let's name him Piddles," suggested Sam, as the brothers all laughed at their brother Gus now covered in dog pee.

41 MEANS TO AN END

The first week in February 1937 passed before the weather cleared enough for Robert and his neighbor Sal to even consider working on Meriden's car in the driveway.

"It's just a few split cores and a small split in the lower radiator tank," said Sal, as he evaluated the damage to Robert's engine and radiator. "I can fix this for you, Robert. Let's pull the radiator out of the car and take it to your workbench in the basement. It's warmer down there!" he said.

"Okay, great! Let's do it...um, looks like six bolts and two hoses. Piece of cake."

"I'll go get my electric solder iron," said Sal as he headed toward his house. "Be right back."

Sal returned minutes later with his electric soldering iron, a roll of lead solder, solder flux paste, a wire brush, and a clear glass gallon bottle filled with a clear liquid.

"What's with the bottle of white lightning, Sal?" asked Meriden as Sal approached the workbench. "Are we gonna celebrate if the radiator don't leak after you fix it?" He was laughing.

"Hardly a bottle of white lightning," Sal answered, grinning. "I will explain more after we get your radiator repaired," he said.

Minutes after warming up the soldering iron, Sal completed a professional repair on Robert's copper radiator cores and tank. Lying on an old blanket, flat on his back under the front end of his car, Meriden connected the lower radiator hose and closed the petcock drain valve.

"Okay, Sal. I think we got her. I'll fetch a pail of water," he said as he crawled out from beneath the car and rose to his feet.

"Only a half pail, Robert," said Sal, pointing to the glass container he'd brought with him.

"Oh yeah, I almost forgot, the bottle of hooch," laughed Robert. "Okay, Sal, you have piqued my curiosity. What the hell is in the bottle?" Robert asked, smiling while rolling his eyes around as a gesture to say what's the big friggin' secret?

Removing the cap from the radiator, Sal began pouring the clear liquid from the glass bottle into the radiator until the bottle was three-fourths empty. "Let's finish this up, and I will explain what this will do. Go ahead and start the motor, Robert. We will top off the radiator with water after it warms up a bit," said Sal.

Once the engine had warmed up, Robert topped off the radiator to the proper fill level, replaced the cap, looked briefly for leaks, and then turned off the motor.

"Absolutely perfect, no leaks! It's perfect…like the day it was built in Michigan," exclaimed Robert. With his right hand on Sal's shoulder, he said, "Thank you, Sal. Now, will you tell me what the heck the big secret is with this bottle?"

With a big grin on his face and moving his head back and forth as if to say no, Sal got very close to Robert's face and quietly said, "It's a secret, Robert. It's a big secret."

"I have spent the last twenty years keeping military secrets—why should this be anything different? What is this liquid anyway? What will it do in my radiator?" asked Robert. "It looks like sugar syrup," he said in a huff.

Sal paused for a moment and explained. "The liquid in the bottle will prevent your radiator and engine block from freezing. You won't have to drain your radiator on freezing winter nights anymore, and yes, it does look like sugar syrup, which is part of the problem.

"Here's the skinny on this stuff, Robert. The liquid in the bottle is called ethylene glycol. It is an ingredient used by a company that manufactures dynamite," said Sal with a smile, knowing this information would raise Robert's eyebrows, and so it did.

"What? Holy smokes," Robert proclaimed. "Is my car going to blow up if I run into a tree or something? I like the idea that it won't freeze but—"

"It's perfectly safe and harmless in your radiator. Don't worry. I would not sabotage you or your car. You just can't drink the stuff," Sal interrupted and explained. "It has not been released for sale to the public yet, so you cannot tell anyone you have it in your car, and most of all, where you got it. *That* is the big secret!

"It is colorless and odorless, so the company is trying to find ways to make it safer for everyone to use before they release it for sale in stores. What's crazy is, somehow they figured out that dogs like to drink this stuff because it is sweet tasting, I guess. They say if you drink as little as four ounces of this chemical it will kill you!"

"What? Four ounces? How did you come by this stuff, Sal?" asked Robert.

"I have a relative who works for a company in South Charleston, West Virginia. He's able to buy this liquid directly from the company...so he tells me. He only comes this way to Rhode Island every so many years, so he brought me a supply to last me until his next visit. I thought this would brighten your day, knowing that you won't have to drain your radiator anymore," Sal said with a big smile. "I can even give you another bottle of the stuff if you want it. I have plenty."

"Yes, I will take it! You have made my day," said Meriden. "Thanks to you and your relative, I have one less thing to worry about this winter!

"Let's get lunch and beers—in *big brown bottles*. I'm buying," Robert boasted.

42 HEADLINING ACT

Word finally came as to where and when Aaron's legendary rock band's final concert event would be—a major venue located on Sunset Boulevard in Los Angeles in just two weeks. How exciting! Because the band was the headlining act, they would, of course, be last on stage late in the evening. My family and I had always supported my son by attending his local shows, and this would not be any different. Normally, however, we would get a nice hotel room near the venue, go to dinner, see the show, and spend the night behaving like rock stars, chillin' with the band before and after the show.

This time, however, Aaron decided that his family needed to show up to this gig *in style*, in a limo dressed like rockers. It was to be a grand evening, so he wanted to share the fun with his family.

No complaints from us. Aaron arranged and paid for both limo and hotel rooms for all of us.

Aaron Rossi—Drummer

43 THE ELIXIR

Over the next two weeks, Robert Meriden practically drove himself crazy contemplating and talking to himself about how to inflict misery and pain onto his nemesis— Giuseppe Rossi.

He was obsessed with crazed thoughts of revenge on the sole person that he believed had destroyed his career, his life, his will to live. Now he even blamed Rossi for his wife Emily's death.

He realized the solution to all his problems was the ethylene glycol. He got the extra bottle from Sal and put it on his kitchen table. He sat staring at the jar of this clear, nondescript lethal liquid for hours.

How can I manipulate someone—whom I've hated and haven't spoken to for nearly a year—to drink this sickening elixir? How?

It's fucking impossible—that's how!

Think, Robert, think—think, man!

I could put it in an empty wine bottle and leave it at the front doo...No, no...someone else might take it. That won't work. Besides, he only drinks homemade wines.

He won't drink gin, but maybe vodka...

No, no...He hates the Russians. It must be in a wine bottle, an Italian wine bottle maybe... damn it...where the hell am I gonna get an Italian wine bottle?

I want the bastard sick and miserable...miserable and sick...enough to want to die, sick and miserable like me, the son of a bitch!

How do you get a fucking mill rat to drink the poison water?

You put in front of him, tempt him, and leave him alone.

44 NIGHTMARE COME TRUE

I t was Friday, March 28. Aaron's LA gig would be in eight days—two nights at the same venue.

I left work in the late afternoon; it had been a long day and a long week in a hot tilt-up concrete building, and I was quite tired and smelly, ready for the weekend. Driving south on the 605 Freeway heading to the 210 East, I cranked up the volume of Aaron's CD that was already playing and started playing the steering wheel drum set.

I caught a glimpse of a guy in a gray Ford Mustang in the lane to the right of me watching me bob my head up and down to the music. I figured he must have thought I was crazy or just showing off. He would not have been entirely wrong on either count. But I really didn't care what he thought—if he had been listening to this music, he would have been bobbing his head too, or not.

Bearing right, taking the two-lane exit onto the 210 East, I chose the left lane. The right lane put drivers immediately into stopping or standing traffic taking the first exit near the Miller brewery. The left lane had its own problem in that it merged with high-speed eastbound motorists.

With nearly completely stopped traffic on my right and high-speed traffic on my left, I cautiously merged into the center lane of eastbound traffic. At the same time, I kept an eye on the vehicle that I was cutting in front of while trying to simultaneously flow at the speed of traffic. Immediately after completing a successful merge, a white vehicle passed closely on my left side; I exchanged glances with the driver and realized that I had seen him before. He had a somewhat angry facial expression, as though I had cut him off. I didn't even know where he'd come from!

Suddenly, without warning, without signals, and with minimal space in front of me, he cut directly in front of me; it was the white cube delivery truck I'd suspected of following me when I'd seen him weeks earlier.

My first instinct was to hit the brakes, but I looked up into my rearview mirror and I had a tractor-trailer on my tail. My foot was on the brake pedal with no pressure applied. I had a wall of white metal doors in front of me. I now had a tractor-trailer at my left rear quarter and a tractor-trailer directly on my right side. I was locked into high-speed traffic, boxed in with large trucks, and I could not slow down. I was feeling completely screwed. Tapping on the brake pedal did not slow the truck behind me.

It seemed like only milliseconds had passed when the clown in front of me made another radical move; this time he moved quickly to the left lane and was gone. Directly in front of me was my all-time worst nightmare: a stopped tractor-trailer with large-diameter bundles of rebar extending off the back of the trailer with little red cloth flags hanging on the end of the bundles.

There was insufficient time to apply the brakes—

When I regained consciousness, it was Sunday noon. I felt a breath in my right ear, someone telling me she loved me—I think. I wasn't sure.

Sedated, delirious, groggy, dry-mouthed, connected to various machines with wires, and with tubes and needles in both arms and an oxygen mask strapped on my face, I could not move my head. I could not move my arms or my legs. My wife was on my right side holding my hand. My son, Aaron, and daughter, Alecia, were at the foot of the bed smiling at me. Aaron was holding back tears; Alecia was crying. There was a doctor—I think—on my left side talking to me, but most of it was a blur.

"You have been in an accident, Mr. Rossi. You are in the hospital. We are taking good care of you. Don't worry," the voice said.

Really, no shit, don't worry!? I can't move my head, arms, or legs, my chest hurts, my face hurts…I think…I can't be sure…I can't talk. I have a mask strapped onto my face. Am I paralyzed?

Just then, I remembered what had happened on the freeway and tears began flowing from my eyes.

45 THE PLAN ENACTED

Wednesday, February 17, 1937, approximately 10:00 a.m.

Robert Meriden entered the package store in Apponaug, a neighborhood in central Warwick not far from the Warwick Town Hall. In the store, he selected bottles of gin, vodka, and expensive wines—the type he thought Giuseppe Rossi *would not* consider drinking—five bottles in all.

He had a plan.

Once he had the props he needed, he drove to the American Screw Company located on Stevens Street in Providence, where he parked his car in an inconspicuous place and sat patiently.

Shortly thereafter, he was out of his car, carefully, slowly looking around for anyone who might see him. There was a great deal of noise coming from the open windows of the red brick factory but not a soul in sight in the employee parking area. Rossi's black 1929 Buick was easy to find.

Meriden knew that Rossi always backed the car into the same parking space in the farthest rear corner of the lot as he had for many years. Nothing had changed. When he arrived at the car, he again glanced around to see if anyone else was in the lot. It was a very cold morning, and no one was in the lot or looking out the mill windows, no one.

Reaching into his trouser pocket, he removed a Schrader valve tool, a small knurled brass cylindrical tool with a bit of a forked end on it. Meriden bent down at the right front tire; removed the valve stem cap, and applied the tool to the inner tube valve stem, loosening it *ever so slightly.*

So slightly, in fact, he put spit on his right index finger and applied it to the poppet valve within the stem. Bubbles appeared, verifying the air was leaking from the valve stem. He replaced the cap loosely.

Meriden, back on his feet, quickly looked around, still no one in sight, and put the Schrader valve tool back into his pocket, headed back to his car, and waited.

46 HOME BY THE WEEKEND

March 31, a Monday morning, at approximately 6:20 a.m., I once again began to show signs of consciousness. The attending nurse advised the resident doctor that I had come to and was staying alert. He did not arrive until after his morning briefings at 8:45 a.m.

My immediate family members were not on hand when he arrived, so he filled me in on the extent of my injuries. The attending nurses were not at liberty to discuss these matters with me.

"Good morning, Mr. Rossi. You are an extremely lucky man," he said as he shook my right hand. "I am Dr. Vu Tran. How are you feeling this morning, sir?" he asked.

"I can't move, Doc," I said. "I feel a kind of numbness, but I cannot move. Am I paralyzed, Doctor?" I asked mumbling.

"Amazingly no, you are not paralyzed," he said, staring directly into my eyes. "I got some of the details of your accident when you arrived in the ER. It's amazing we are having this conversation," he said. I could feel my eyes welling up with tears as he spoke.

"You suffered a traumatic event, a car accident last Friday. You were brought here by ambulance early evening, unconscious. Your breathing was shallow and erratic. You were clammy, lips were blue, pulse weak. You did not look good.

"We did a full workup on you—x-rays, oxygen, intravenous drip, blood work, checked for internal bleeding. You became conscious for a brief period, however we believed you were in a state of physiological shock. You were agitated and confused.

"During the time you were unconscious, we immobilized you to protect you from yourself. That is why you cannot move.

"You again passed out until Sunday and became conscious around noontime, and then passed out again shortly thereafter. Your family and our nursing staff have monitored you around the clock since your arrival here.

"You have bruising from the seatbelt restraint across your chest. Your eyes were irritated from the powder that released from the air bag deployment. Your face has some minor abrasions. All things considered, you are in great shape!" he said with an enthusiastic smile.

Still slightly sedated, I choked for words but managed to say, "Thank you, Doctor, thank you."

"We will remove the restraints you have on and monitor you for the next few days. You should be able to go home by the weekend."

47 THE ACT COMMITTED

Day-shift workers began to leave the plant and arrive in the parking lot area at 2:35 p.m. Robert Meriden had sampled the bottled beverages he'd bought earlier in the day and now had an urgent need to relieve himself.

In the immediate area behind his car, Meriden was blissfully watering the weeds when a fine young female worker passed by.

"Like what you see, sweetheart?" he asked

She pointed at his penis and yelled, "Needle Dick," and then ran to her car laughing hysterically all the way.

Meriden finished his business and angrily got back into the car.

After a difficult day inside the mill, Giuseppe Rossi lumbered into the parking lot at 3:05 p.m., climbed into his car, and began his forty-five-minute drive home.

Minutes into his journey, he realized there was a problem with the front of the car and pulled off the road to the right side shoulder. The right front tire was almost completely flat. Without hesitating, Rossi began to unfasten the spare tire. Just then, a car pulled up behind Rossi's Buick.

"Hello, Mr. Rossi. Can I lend a hand to my old friend?" asked Meriden.

Giuseppe looked up thinking it was Mariano from the plant and was surprised to see Robert Meriden standing before him instead.

"My goodness, they let anybody drive on the roads these days...and I'm not that old," replied Rossi with a laugh. The two men shook hands.

Meriden jacked the car up while Rossi removed the lug bolts. Together they made the tire exchange in five minutes flat.

"Let me buy you a drink, Giuseppe. I owe you that," said Meriden.

"I owe you for stopping to help me, but I really just want to get home. I'm tired and hungry...just pulled a double shift. I have to pass on the drink offer," explained Rossi.

"I just came from downtown. I have wine, gin, vodka, and glasses on the front seat of my car...come on, try something new. I had some—it's great!" he boasted.

"Okay, one quick glass and I got to get home," Rossi said, knowing it was the quickest way to get away from Meriden.

Meriden grabbed the bottle of wine with the fancy label he had previously opened and filled his own glass and then attempted to pour some into the glass that Giuseppe was now holding.

"I don't want to drink up your expensive wines. What are the clear bottles in the backseat?" Rossi asked.

"Some homemade hooch I got from my West Virginia relative a last week…it's smooth. Can you tell I sampled of that too?"

"Pour me a glass from the opened bottle—let me try the homemade hooch" said Rossi.

Meriden filled Giuseppe's empty glass. "One glass of hooch coming up."

"Here's to old friends," said Rossi

Giuseppe smelled the concoction first and then drank it down as Meriden watched.

"Well that's different. It is smooth…a little sweet…somewhat odd actually." He smiled. "Let me try another glass. Maybe it will taste better if I have more."

"I don't want to be responsible for you driving home drunk and getting in trouble with your missus," said Meriden, pretending as if he cared.

"One more glass won't kill me. Okay…okay…I won't drink it now. I'll take it home with me for later. Call it one for the road!"

Meriden gladly refilled the empty glass.

48 EYEWITNESS ACCOUNTS

On Friday, April 4, at 11:30 a.m., an orderly rolled me out of my hospital room into the hallway.

Looking down the hall to the left at the nurse's station, I caught a glimpse of Dr. Tran speaking to a man with a long gray-haired ponytail wearing a denim jacket with a combat soldier silhouette on his back, similar to the ones I'd seen in Rhode Island.

Must be a national organization.

We turned right, toward the elevators, down to the hospital front entrance; I managed to walk, however stiffly and sorely, to the car on my own.

Although I'd had the greatest of care at the hospital, I was ready for some home cooking, my own bed, and my own shower.

At home on the kitchen table were accident report copies that my wife had obtained from the insurance company. There were three eyewitness accounts of the accident, one of which was an off-duty plainclothes police officer. Each witness had the same story. They all saw the white delivery vehicle cut in front of me, then cut out immediately, and the stopped tractor-trailer with its overextended load of rebar. There was nothing in front of the tractor-trailer and no reason for it to be completely stopped in the middle of the freeway.

The off-duty police officer stated, "It was actually the overextended rebar that prevented a fatal accident." He reasoned that the "rebar absorbed the majority force of the impact"; additionally, the "shoulder-lap belt helped to minimize contact forces with the exterior of the vehicle."

Apparently, the front of my truck struck two of the three hanging bundles of steel that folded under the front of my truck, preventing me from going under the trailer. The third bundle slid across the top of my hood and crashed through the windshield on the passenger side of the vehicle. The tractor-trailer that was close behind me plowed into my rear bumper, pushing me further into the front trailer. My pick-up was folded in the middle. I was pinned in the front seat. Rescue members extracted me from the wreck using the Jaws of Life.

Had I had a passenger in the vehicle, the outcome would have been tragic.

The rebar truck driver attempted to flee the accident scene; however, my pick-up was stuck to the rebar attached to the bed of the trailer. He did not get far.

The big rig behind me also attempted to leave the scene but was followed by a witness who informed police by cell phone; he did not get far either.

A highway patrol officer's report amended to the insurance paperwork claimed that arrests were made in connection to the accident and that the "suspicious nature" of the accident was pending investigation.

Suspicious nature?

Arrests?

The tractor's engine had stalled…I thought.

There were clearly no statements that indicated I was at fault in this accident—that was good, at least!

I am sincerely grateful to those who came to my aid in my time of need.

Thank you to the witnesses who came forward.

Thank you to the off-duty police officer that went beyond the call of duty.

You saved my life.

48 TWO FAMILIES DEVASTATED

Giuseppe arrived home at 4:15 p.m., exhausted and suddenly not feeling well. The sun was nearly gone for the day, and it was becoming very cold indeed. Vincenza had water boiling for pasta on the stove; it was warm in the kitchen. Giuseppe removed his work boots and heavy jacket in the entry hall.

"I'm going to rest for a few minutes before dinner, if that's okay. I'm not feeling well," he explained.

"You must be exhausted, my dear husband. I will wake you when dinner is ready," she said as she kissed him on the cheek.

Still carrying the glass of hooch, Giuseppe set the glass on the nightstand beside the bed and lay down.

At 5:00 p.m., Giuseppe felt nauseous. He got up to get the washbowl on top of the dresser and began vomiting and dry heaving. He was perspiring, weak, and had difficulty breathing. He had never felt so awful.

"Must have caught the flu," he reasoned to himself. Feeling too weak to call for Vincenza, he lay back down onto the bed and fell unconscious.

Maria Angelina stopped by to say hello to her parents on her way home from work and dropped off a freshly baked loaf of Italian bread.

"Your papa is upstairs sleeping, sweetheart. He had a drink on the way home, and I think it knocked him out. He was so tired, the poor thing. I need to go wake him for dinner," Vincenza said as she started to remove her apron.

"I will go upstairs and wake him, Mama. You stay here," Maria said as she proceeded to the next room and up the stairs to the second floor.

When she opened the door to the bedroom, it smelled terrible. Giuseppe was on the bed unconscious, perspiring heavily and struggling to breathe.

"Poor man must be sick," she thought. "He needs his rest."

Beside the bed on the nightstand was the glass of illicit hooch.

"He must have drank this alcohol to help him sleep," she thought.

Maria picked up the glass and sniffed the contents. There was no smell.

"I could use a good night's sleep too," she thought. "Papa won't mind if I sample his sleep medicine—he certainly doesn't need any more of it," she reasoned.

Maria drank half of the glass's contents; it was so sweet on her palate that she dropped the glass on the floor and it broke.

She first looked to see if she had disturbed her father, but he did not move. Reaching down to pick up the broken glass, she cut her right thumb and index finger; they began to bleed. She picked up the broken shard of glass with her left hand and the glass itself with her right hand and then headed back to the kitchen.

"Let Papa sleep a while—I think he may be sick," Maria explained to her mother as she poured the remaining hooch into the kitchen sink and onto her cut fingers, thinking the alcohol would disinfect the wounds. Reaching into a drawer to the right of the sink were some clean white dishtowels; she wrapped her bleeding fingers in the towel.

"I will check on him later. Stay for some pasta," insisted Vincenza.

"No, no, I must get home to make dinner for my family, Mama—take care of Papa. I will come tomorrow to see how he is. I love you, Mama!" She headed out the door and into the cold.

"Love you too, sweetheart," answered Vincenza.

At 7:10 p.m. Vincenza finished cleaning the kitchen and headed upstairs to check on her husband.

He was still, not making a sound—not snoring as usual. She shook him at his shoulder. His clothing was soaking wet.

"Papa…Papa…Papa!"

At 10:45 p.m. the phone rang in the kitchen of the Rossi residence. Nicholas Rossi answered the phone. Maria Angelina had succumbed to the same fate as her father.

Giuseppe Rossi of Natick, age fifty-one and father of nine children, and Maria Angelina Stabile, of Norwood, age twenty-eight and mother of three children, were dead.

Dr. G. Senerchia declared that cause of death was "lobar pneumonia."

Giuseppe's body was taken to Prata Undertaking Company.

Dr. Luigi Maiello also declared that cause of death was "lobar pneumonia."

Maria's body was taken John Di Orio & Sons Undertaker.

On February 18, 1937, at 7:50 a.m., Nicholas Rossi stepped outside into the cold morning air to collect his thoughts. He and his six brothers had been up all night with their mother; he was physically and mentally exhausted as were they all.

He sat briefly on the cement front step and looked to his right in the direction of the garage. The garage door was open.

"Papa would never leave that door opened," he thought. Nicholas stepped into the garage and looked around briefly; everything was in its place, until he got to the corner of the garage where the Flying Torpedo had hung for the past eighteen years. It was gone. The base was there, but the prototype was missing.

Devastated, tired, and too overwhelmed to give it much thought, Nicholas closed the door and went back into the house.

Immediately following the burial of their father and sister, the Rossi brothers held a family meeting; Nicholas, the oldest, spoke to his brothers.

"I realize we just buried Papa, and Sis, but we need to decide how we are going to support Mama, ourselves, and keep the house that Papa built for us.

"No one else is going to help us. We do not have any rich relatives, and Mama has never had a job. It is up to us, us alone."

Anthony, the youngest, began to cry, and then Gennaro. "I want my Papa. I want my Papa," cried Anthony.

It was the Depression era; work was scarce, especially for young men without specific skills.

Lawrence, age fifteen, got a job at Lindy's Diner in Cranston. He worked six days a week, twelve hours a day. His salary was twelve dollars per week. He paid someone to drive him there daily; the remaining money went to his mother.

Giuseppe paid for Augustino to attend electrician school; he became an apprentice. He later worked at Quonset Point.

Michael worked at Pelkie's Truck Garage, sawing oak wood by hand for truck bodies.

Gennaro, age thirteen, went to work in Natick Mills as a cloth inspector and machine operator.

Nicholas could not find work immediately but later worked at Quonset Point.

50 A KINDNESS RETURNED

uring the last weekend in May 1937, Father Tirrochi took his baseball team to Natick Field for a Saturday afternoon game. The Rossi boys went to meet their neighborhood friends and catch the game.

A few innings into the game, Gennaro realized that some of the boys participating in the game were his former classmates at school. Although he worked in the mill with boys his age, he wished he could be on the team; he wished his Papa were still alive, he wished...

Father Tirrochi with the Natick Baseball Team

Gennaro sat on a nearby bench and began to cry.

Delia, Rita, and Bertha of the Beron family children were at the field as well. Rita Beron spotted Gennaro on the bench, walked over, and sat beside him. She put her arm around his shoulder and proceeded to console Gennaro until he stopped crying, as he had done for her two years earlier.

Six years quickly past, Gennaro, age nineteen, entered the United States Army on March 23, 1943, in the city of Providence. He completed basic training at Fort Devens, Massachusetts, and was later sent to participate in the war efforts taking place in Northern France.

Attached to Company K 424th Infantry Regiment, PFC Gennaro J. Rossi fought in the Rhineland Conflict and was decorated with the Good Conduct Medal, Victory Medal, European African Middle Eastern Theater Campaign Ribbon, and the American Theater Campaign Ribbon. Rita Beron corresponded by letter to Gennaro during the course of the war.

PFC Gennaro J. Rossi
Rifle Marksman

Rossi brothers Samuel, Anthony, Lawrence, and Nicholas enlisted into the United States Armed Forces as well.

Samuel Rossi, in the United States Navy, served in Europe.

Anthony Rossi, in the United States Army, served in Japan.

Lawrence Rossi, in the United States Coast Guard, transported troops and supplies throughout Europe and Africa and brought back German prisoners of war.

Nicholas Rossi, in the United States Army, served within the United States.

Vincenza Rossi kept five stars in her window, which meant she had five sons in the war.

Augustino and Michael assisted with the war effort at home, which was a huge comfort to their mother.

Gennaro "Jerry' Rossi

Lawrence "Larry" Rossi   Nicholas "Nick" Rossi

Antonio "Tony" Rossi

Samuel "Sam" Rossi

Michael "Mike" Rossi

Augustino "Gus" Rossi

During this time period, Robert Meriden II, now age thirty-three (he had begun his military career in 1929), had already served fourteen years of his career in the United States Army and wanted to retire with twenty years under his belt.

The younger Meriden moved into his father's house, taking over the main house to raise his own family; Meriden Sr. moved into the apartment above the garage.

Meriden II felt it was necessary to keep an eye on his father, who was now a belligerent alcoholic. He had become a danger to himself and those around him.

Meriden II would complete his career in the army working locally in the city of Providence with brief periods in the War Department located in Washington, DC.

51 SOLDIERS RETURN

It was August 3, 1945, and Gennaro Rossi was happy to be back on US soil.

Mom, brothers, neighbors, and friends were on hand at his mother's house where he received a hero's welcome, as each of his brothers received when they returned home.

It was a joyous time to celebrate. For them, and the rest of the world, the war was finally over.

When the festivities concluded at home, Gennaro went directly to the Beron residence to see Rita Beron.

An inevitable courtship ensued, followed by a marriage proposal. The wedding date was set for the third week in February.

Beron Residence, East Natick Avenue

Rita Beron and Gennaro Rossi

52 SHREDDER RETURNS

Saturday morning, April 5, I awoke feeling like I had been run over twice by one of those pick-up trucks with big nobby tires. However nothing was going to stop me from attending Aaron's show that night. He had been on tour for seven months around the United States and parts of Europe. They were the headlining band that night and were slated to be on stage at 10:00 p.m. It seemed strange that Aaron wanted us there "a bit early." I guessed he'd missed us just like we'd missed him.

Jan and I spent the afternoon getting our concert outfits on—basically black on black. We had not heard from Alecia, but she was due to be at our house to ride with us to the venue.

The limousine arrived on schedule at 7:00 p.m. sharp; the professionally dressed, well-mannered driver introduced himself as Javier.

Alecia finally arrived at 7:11 p.m., which meant our very punctual limo driver was still set on getting us to the gig on time. With a few of my curious neighbors looking on, the three of us climbed into the limo. We were looking and feeling like rockstars.

Heading north on the 405 Freeway, we proceeded to Los Angeles. I could not help but notice the driver being distracted by something in his rearview mirror, as I was sitting in the rear seat facing forward. Using the "Driver"call button located on the armrest, I asked Javier if there was a problem with the car.

"No, no, Señor. There is a car following us," he reported. "Do you have more family to ride in the limo?" he asked.

"No, Javier, no more family members. What kind of a car is it?" I asked.

"A gray Mustang, Señor, with two men in it," he said.

No one but a few of my close neighbors even know we are in this car. Is it possible we are actually being followed?

I informed the driver, "It's not anyone we know, Javier. Please do not stop."

178

We entered the arena grounds where lines of fans had organized to enter the turnstiles into the concert hall. Security guards made an open passage for the limo to pass through the lines and drive close to the Will Call window. It was necessarry for us to exit the limo and walk up to the window to show proper identification to get our entry passes, backstage passes with neck strap, hand stamps, and wrist bands.

I was beginning to think they would take a blood sample for DNA and have us pee in a cup for good measure.

Javier directed us to return to the limo. We proceeded to a side entrance with a large metal rollup overhead door. He tooted the car horn and the metal door opened. He drove the limo inside the arena. The large metal door closed quickly as Javier held the car door while we exited the limo.

Arena personel with yellow T-shirts that had SECURITY in large black letters on their back escorted Jan, Alecia, and myself inside to the seating area. We were positioned in an area devoid of seats. I did not wish to stand all evening, but there had to be a reason we had been brought to that spot. I just did not know what that reason was.

People were being allowed into the the auditorium, and it was filling quickly. One of the opening acts, Sonic Syndicate, was on stage annoying the audience with their trashy techno rock.

Just then a young man with all the same security garb, with curly hair and a beard, walked up to me and asked, "Mr. Rossi?"

"Yes, who are you, sir?"

"My name is Josh. Aaron asked that I bring you back stage to the warm-up studio. Could you please come with me?" he asked politely.

"Just me, not the family?" I asked.

"Just you," said Josh. "I think he needs help with his kit," he added. *This is all very strange. Oh well, let's see what Aaron is up to.*

Josh and I entered an inner service hallway where he had a two-seater electric cart with two chrome exaust pipes bolted on the roof. Folks scattered as he raced to the rear of the building, tooting the squeaky horn most of the way.

Josh stopped in front of an unmarked door and asked me to go inside. I opened the door only to find another door three feet inside of the first.

"Mr. Rossi, please close the outer door so that you can open the inner door," Josh advised.

"Thanks, Josh!"

53 CIGARS CAN KILL

On Saturday, February 16, 1946, at 7:15 a.m., Henry Beron went to his cigar store to pick up boxes of cigars for the wedding. This would only take a moment, he thought, as he unlocked the front entrance door, leaving it open wide enough to let light in to see inside the store.

As Henry had his back to the street as he was unlocking the door, Robert Meriden drove past and saw Henry enter the cigar store. Meriden had his small fishing boat in tow. He made an instant U-turn and parked in front of Henry's store.

Henry came out of the storeroom at the back of the store only to find a large figure of a man in his doorway. He could not tell who it was; the blinding sun was rising behind him.

"Sorry, sir, we are closed this morning," announced Henry. "I was just—"

"Henry, it's me, Robert Meriden."

Henry had not seen Robert Meriden in his store since Giuseppe Rossi passed away.

"Hello, Robert. Long time no see," said Henry, "What can I—"

"Oh, been busy, ya know. Hey, I was just going fishing. I sure could use a couple boxes of them short Panatelas—whatta ya say?"

Henry could smell an odor of alcohol on Meriden's breath. He was unbathed and unshaved.

"Okay, Robert, but then I got to lock up and get out of here," said Henry as he once again proceeded to the rear storeroom.

When he returned, Robert Meriden was staring at an old newspaper clipping tacked on the wall. "Robot Planes? A Natick Man Flew One in R.I. in 1918," Robert read aloud. "That Nazi-loving fascist bastard, I took care of that son of bitch," he said under his breath.

Henry heard exactly what Meriden had just mumbled; however, he pretended he hadn't. "I'm a bit hard of hearing, Robert. What did you say?" asked Henry as he handed Meriden his cigars.

"Oh...aaa...aaa, strange how old Rossi up and died all of a sudden, eh?" stammered Meriden.

Although he tried not to show it, Henry felt himself becoming hot under the collar. Giuseppe had been his friend after all, and for some unknown reason, he suspected Meriden had something to do with his sudden death.

"Are you aware that Maria Angelina died that very same day, a few hours after visiting her father, in fact?" Henry asked Meriden.

Meriden's face suddenly turned bright red. His eyes began to well up with tears.

"Oh my, oh my, no...I was unaware of that. I...didn't know," slurred Meriden.

Henry did not know how Meriden had been involved with Giuseppe and Angelina's deaths, but he was even more convinced that he had been after this conversation.

"Let me show you to the door, Robert. I really need to lock up now and get going," Henry said as he escorted Meriden to the front entrance.

Henry locked the front door of the shop and walked down the stairs to the sidewalk. Robert Meriden had his car door open. As Henry passed by, he noticed a bottle of whiskey and a handgun on the front seat.

Henry was practically blind and not physically capable of driving an automobile, so he walked down the hill on Main Street toward his house. Robert Meriden passed him by in his car towing the boat and smoking a cigar.

As Henry walked across the bridge on East Avenue, he spotted Meriden on the east side of the bridge unloading his boat into the Pawtuxet Valley River.

Stopping briefly at home to check on Rita, the bride to be, he then walked to Vincenza Rossi's house where the Rossi brothers were all getting prepared for Gennaro's wedding day.

Compelled yet reluctant to say anything, Henry waited for the opportunity to get all the brothers outside, except Gennaro, and explained to them his verbal encounter with Robert Meriden at the cigar shop. He also told them where they could find Meriden.

Nicholas stepped back into the house briefly, and then the six brothers got into two cars and proceeded to the East Natick Bridge.

Main Street Natick

Henry went into the house, poured himself a cup of coffee, sat down at the kitchen table, and contemplated his actions.

Gennaro was admiring his tuxedo in the mirror when he suddenly realized how quiet it was downstairs. His brothers generally made more noise when they got together than a house full of women. He stepped into the hallway and peered out the front window in time to see his brothers speeding away in their cars.

"What the hell's going on?" he said aloud as he ran down the staircase and on into the kitchen where Henry Beron was sitting.

"Mr. Beron?"

"Jerry...please call me Henry," he responded, smiling. "We will be related to each other in a few short hours."

"What just happened here, Henry? Where did my brothers race off to?" asked Gennaro.

Henry began tapping on the table with his fingernails as he always did when he was thinking of what to say next.

"I have known you since I was a child, Henry, and you have never lied to me...please do not lie to me now. What is going on?" pleaded Gennaro.

"Yes, that is true. Very well," Henry said as he began explaining what was transpiring.

Gennaro ran to the cellar door, opened it, and blindly reached around the corner searching for something.

"Dammit," he said as he closed the door and headed out the front door.

Henry Beron

54 JUST WARMING UP

Entering the warm-up studio, I found Aaron and Sammy (the lead guitarist) discussing the set list.

"Heeey, Dad. Thanks for coming. You know Sammy?" Aaron asked.

"Yes, of course. How are you, Sammy?" I asked.

"I'm great, Mr. Rossi. Heard you were in a bad accident last week. How are you feeling?" Sammy asked.

"Just glad to be among the living," I answered with a big smile. "Did you need me for something?" I asked, turning to Aaron.

"Yes, Dad. Could you please try out this electric kit for me? My tech is not here yet, and Sammy wants to do a few licks to be sure the kit amps don't interfere with the lead amps. It will only take a few minutes. I need to get dressed to go on stage," he said.

"Ha! I haven't played in many, many years. Sammy, are you sure?" I asked preapologizing for what was about to take place.

"Oh, hell yes. Please, if you don't mind," Sammy said.

"Okay, let's do this," I said as I took a pair of Aaron's signature drumsticks from him.

"Put these headphones on, Dad. It is super noisy in this small room. These will help you to hear yourself and Sammy perfectly. I gotta go," said Aaron as he departed.

I made a few necessary adjustments to the kit and began to play double bass, double toms, double floor toms, crash, ride, and hi-hat. Sammy began picking some awesome lead riffs, and suddenly, we were jammin'!

55 BRIDGE OVER THE PAWTUXET

ix Rossi brothers stood on the concrete East Natick Bridge looking down at Robert Meriden who was babbling and crying uncontrollably. His small green wooden boat in the calm waters did not appear to be anchored; an uncast fishing pole stuck out of the front of the boat.

He had a revolver in his right hand resting on his right leg and a bottle of whiskey in the left.

Startled by the appearance of the Rossi brothers standing a few feet above him, he calmly placed the bottle of whiskey between his shoes and scooted his feet tightly to hold it there. Slowly he raised the revolver he had in his right hand and pressed it firmly against his right temple.

"I didn't know...I didn't know she...she...I'm sorry—" Meriden babbled. "I will end this...now," he said.

It then appeared as though he was about to pull the trigger.

Seeing the firearm Meriden was holding, Nicholas reached into his pocket and slowly pulled out a Luger 9mm semiautomatic firearm that had once belonged to his father. He kept it concealed low behind the concrete bridge sidewall as protection for himself and his brothers.

"Robert Meriden, put that gun down before you hurt yourself and get your drunk ass up here. You have some explaining to do," Nicholas firmly demanded.

Meriden was motionless. Staring straight ahead into the ripples of the water, whimpering softly—seemingly forever, but really only for a second.

Michael became impatient with Meriden's inaction and grabbed the Luger from Nicholas's hand. He was trembling with extreme anger, but he also kept it concealed.

"What did you do to our father, you piece of shit? Our sister?" screamed Michael. "We are taking you to the police station."

Samuel then took the revolver from Michael's trembling hand. He too kept it concealed from Meriden. He realized Meriden had been drinking already and did not wish to provoke him.

Meriden looked up at the Rossi brothers with disdain and anger and began yelling at them.

"*You fffuckers are all still too fucking young and too fffucking stupid to understand...the man ruined my marriage...he ruined my fucking military career...that...killed...my wife! Do you fffucking understand? He and that flying fucking torpedo ruined my entire fffuckin' life. You just cannot possibly fucking understand! You fucking...fucking idiots!*"

"Our father admired you, Meriden! He completely trusted you with his patent as a friend...like a brother!" claimed Samuel solemnly.

Augustino took the revolver from Samuel's hand, but kept it concealed. "Enough of this bullshit talk—"

"You murdered our sister too. Do you know you killed our sister, you son of bitch? She had three kids and a husband. She drank the same shit you gave our father."

Lawrence calmly reached over and took the Luger from Augustino. He kept it concealed, but he aligned it and was ready to fire at Meriden if the situation changed.

"You had no right to kill our father and sister, Meriden," he said in a peaceful tone. "It's time to make restitution."

"*You fuckers don't have the fucking balls. None of ya. No balls!*" yelled Meriden, and then he smiled. "*You don't even have a fucking weapon, ya bunch of fucking dumb-asses.*"

Antonio grabbed his brother Lawrence's arm and pulled the Luger from his hand. He kept it below Meriden's sight level. "I want my father and sister back," said Antonio angrily as he pulled the slide back on the weapon to load a round into the firing chamber.

Meriden, a trained military man himself, heard the slide action. He also saw the anger and determination in Antonio's eyes and immediately felt threatened. He raised his revolver in the direction of Antonio and fired two rounds. Both bullets hit the concrete bridge sidewall on either side of Antonio, sending bits of concrete into Antonio's eyes.

He then pulled the hammer back and took aim to deliver a third bullet at Antonio—the kill shot.

Antonio blindly raised his hand to return fire.

Another single shot rang out. A loud cracking sound, different from the two Meriden had just fired.

Robert Meriden flew backward into his boat.

The handgun he held fell into the water and submerged into the thick mud below. The bottle of whiskey sitting on the boat bottom had not moved. The boat began to drift aimlessly downstream.

The Rossi brothers all looked toward their youngest brother Antonio with their mouths agape in disbelief.

Standing next to Antonio was the fresh-out-of-combat veteran Gennaro Rossi in his tuxedo. He had snatched the Luger from the hand of his baby brother Antonio with such precision that Antonio had not realized he was no longer holding the weapon in his own hand.

Gennaro had fired the single shot with his left hand to protect his brothers and himself from the suicidal and crazed Meriden.

In that reactive-fleeting moment, Gennaro was in a different mind-set, a distant place—back on the battlefield, instinctively returning fire when fired upon—in self-defense.

Gennaro watched as the boat floated away from the bridge down river. "It was meant to be a patent for prosperity, not a patent for murder!" he exclaimed, as though Meriden could possibly still hear him.

"And no one shoots at my baby brother—on my wedding day, damn it—or at least not before breakfast," exclaimed Gennaro.

Gennaro then placed the Luger inside the tuxedo jacket and turned to his brothers. "I thought the war was over," he said solemnly. Gennaro placed his right hand on his brother Antonio's shoulder, smiled at him, and said, "Were you just gonna let that guy use you for target practice or what? Are you all right, little brother?"

"But…but—" Antonio stammered to reply. "Ye-yes, I'm OK," he replied, brushing bits of concrete from his eyelashes.

The brothers all laughed. "Are you OK?" Nicholas asked Gennaro, as his brothers gathered around him, each putting one hand on his shoulder.

Gennaro was silent.

Glancing into each brother's eyes, he was grateful none of them were harmed.

He nodded to them, "Yes, I am OK."

"Henry's back at the house making crepes and bacon for us—who's hungry?" asked Gennaro as he climbed into Samuel's car, knowing his brothers were still traumatized.

The brothers stood still and looked at where Gennaro had been standing; there was Nicholas's old bicycle from the garage.

"I love Henry's crepes," said Mike.

"Me too," said Augustino. "With bacon."

"Tony, take my bicycle back to the garage, and I will save you a crepe," said Nicholas, smiling.

"And some bacon," yelled Antonio.

"Bacon? What? No Italian sausage?" asked Larry.

"Today is turning out to be a glorious day," Sam said sincerely to Gennaro as he drove off the bridge.

"Yeah, I like Henry's crepes too," said Gennaro as he and his brothers laughed all the way home.

Gennaro Rossi

February 16, 1946
Newlyweds—Gennaro and Rita Rossi

It's so important to make someone happy.
Make just one someone happy,
Make just one heart the heart you, you sing to.
One smile that cheers you,
One face that lights when it nears you,
One girl you're ev'rything to. Fame, if win it,
Comes and goes in a minutes.
Where's the real stuff in life to cling to?
Love is the answer.
Someone to love is the answer.
Once you've found her,
Build your world around her.
Make someone happy.
Make just one someone happy.
And you will be happy too.

—Jimmy Durante, 1965

Henry Beron, Rita (Beron) Rossi, Gennaro Rossi

189

56 WE WILL ROCK YOU

ammy and I had been jamming for less than five minutes when Aaron came back into the room. I stopped playing and removed the headphones. Suddenly I could here what sounded like an audience screaming and laughing. "What's that, Aaron?" I asked.

"Oh...uh...that's a sound feed from the main stage so we know what is happening out there in real time...sounds like the second opening act the Down Beats is on stage.

"Wow, you guys sounded great, Dad. I could hear you while I was getting dressed," Aaron complimented.

Showing off a bit, I kicked the double bass pedals, boom boom, bah... boom boom bah...singing into the microphone, "Kicking your can all over the place," boom boom, bah...

Then from the sound feed I heard, "We will we will rock you...We will we will rock you..."

I looked at Aaron and Sammy. "What the—?"

I heard the boom boom, bah as I hit the bass pedals again and then, "We will we will rock you...We will we will rock you...," from the sound feed.

"They love you, Dad," Aaron said as he pointed to a small camera attached high up on the wall.

Slightly embarrassed, I did not know whether to laugh or cry. I handed Aaron back his drumsticks. "Thank you, Sammy! That was amazing. I'm gonna get back to your mom and sister, Aaron. Hope to see you after the show!"

"Thanks, Dad, of course. Josh is waiting outside to take you back. I am going to send two of our finest personal security people, Dozzer and Freight Train, to keep your new fans from bothering you and Mom and Lee. Enjoy the show!" he said as I walked out of the studio.

Back inside the auditorium, there was not an empty seat in the house. Josh escorted me back to where Jan and Alecia were. It appeared that Javier had decided to return to the limo. The Down Beats were finishing their last song. The stage curtain closed. In the interim, there was prerecorded music playing.

Good time to go pee.

I turned around to navigate a path through the crowd to the restroom. Behind Jan and me were two very large well-dressed men. I assumed they were Dozzer and Freight Train. I nodded to them to acknowledge their presence. I could not talk to them—the music was simply too loud.

Behind them was another pair of large, scary-looking, heavily tatted men, both wearing black t-shirts.

Thank goodness Dozzer and Freight Train are here.

Just then the loud music subsided, the master of ceremonies was on stage, and the curtain began to open. The MC thanked Sonic Syndicate and the Down Beats for their performance and promised to bring out the headliners, Diablo.

"But first," he said, "we have a special guest in our audience. Someone dear to us almost did not make it to the show tonight because of an accident just this past week." He turned and pointed to the large projection screen behind him.

There on the big screen was a picture of my truck. Crumpled in half, the driver's side door missing—I could hardly bear to look at it.

I was motionless. I put my dark glasses back on as tears streamed from eyes. Jan and Alecia each grabbed my hands and squeezed tightly.

At that moment, Diablo's drummer, Aaron Rossi, stepped onto the stage. The audience went crazy cheering. The MC handed him the microphone.

"Ladies and gentlemen, my dad was in that truck," said Aaron, who could barely speak as he pointed to the big screen.

The audience fell silent. You could hear a pin drop.

"But he's here tonight! I love you, Dad!"

Just then, a video started to play on the big screen.

"Heeey, Dad. Thanks for coming." They had recorded video of me walking into the sound room and jamming with Sammy on the drums. It was kind of funny actually.

As the music Sammy and I were playing on the video became progressively louder, I realized there was commotion all around us and a ruckus of major proportion was taking place behind us.

Suddenly a feeling came over me that something bad was about to happen.

Jan and I got pushed hard to the floor from behind—pushed, not bumped.

I turned around as quickly as I could to ask Jan and Alecia if they were okay. They were both fine.

New fans my ass—didn't these clowns see the picture of my truck? Dammit that hurt! We must be in the center of the friggin mosh pit.

I'm gonna mosh them…Whoa…Shit.

The two well-dressed men that had been standing behind us were now on the floor. The two burley-tattooed guys were standing over them. It said Security in white letters on the back of their black T-shirts. Dozzer? Freight Train?

Surrounding them were at least six men in black suits with earpieces in their ears, two of which were pulling out handcuffs from under the suit jackets to cuff the two guys on the floor.

I don't get it. What just happened here?

Dozzer…Freight Train?

The audience was crazy with excitement. The entire disturbance—caught on camera—was now being displayed on the big screen. The audience thought it was part of the show.

Just then, as if things couldn't get crazier, the MC announced, "Ladies and Germs, Boys and Girls, I give you Diablo!"

The band opened up with their latest number-one hit single "(Shaped Like An Hourglass) She's My Black Widow Lover," which brought the house to its feet!

Everyone around us was singing the lyrics to the song. There was electricity in the air—and a tap on my right shoulder.

"Señor Rossi…Señor Rossi, un minuto por favor," said a familiar voice from behind me.

"Mr. Rossi, my name is Javier Ojinaga. I'm an undercover agent with Homeland Security," said Javier smiling, with absolutely no accent, holding his identification wallet in hand.

Dozzer and Freight Train formally introduced themselves to me as well. Standing with Javier was three additional men in black suits wearing earpieces—plus Dozzer and Freight Train.

This is crazy. Am I dreaming?

"This will only take a moment of your time. May we escort you and your family to a quieter place so we may speak, or would you prefer stay here?" he asked.

My anchors, Jan and Alecia, clinging firmly to each arm, held me steadfast in place.

I looked at Dozzer standing to my left and Freight Train on my right; they both motioned with their fingers pointing to the floor to indicate that I should stay there.

"We would like to stay here, Agent Ojinaga. Are we in some sort of danger?" I asked.

"You *were* in serious danger, Mr. Rossi. You are completely safe now," he said, as people all around us were "moshing" to the rock music.

"Serious danger?"

"I was assigned to your case after your accident last week, sir. It was not an accident, rather an attempt on your life."

"My case?"

"Six individuals, including two this evening who were armed with knives, have been arrested and taken into custody, as well as three men in Warwick, Rhode Island, following our investigation into this incident. All are charged with attempted murder," Javier explained.

"Attempted murder? Me? My family? For what reason?"

"You were investigated by Homeland Security post-911 for Internet searches you made regarding weapons of mass destruction," he said.

"Yes, I suspected that. I have been writing a book about my grandfather," I replied.

"Nothing became of that investigation, until *you* showed up in Warwick, Rhode Island, at a home of suspected illegal small arms dealer."

Just then, Diablo finished one song and immediately began playing another. The audience was applauding, screaming, moshing to the music.

"I'm sorry, Javier—did you say 'small arms dealer'?" I asked in disbelief. "Who possibly can that be?"

"You were seen by our agents at the residence of one Robert Meriden," he said, handing me a photo of me inside the biker garage in Warwick.

"I was there seeking information about my grandfather from Robert Meriden the Second. I was told that he'd passed away by this biker working in the garage," I said, pointing to the individual in the photograph.

"That man *is* Robert Meriden...*the Third*, the son of Robert Meriden the Second. He apparently ordered a contract hit on your life. He and his cronies have been arrested and are being held for the attempted murder of you and your family."

"For what reason, Javier? I still don't understand," I said, bewildered.

"In an effort to protect his grandfather and his father's reputations as honorable soldiers—an investigation of them may have proved otherwise.

"Meriden and his associates are under investigation for selling small arms. Whatever you said to him that day in the garage apparently struck a nerve. You came too close to the Meriden family secret.

"Our Boston office thoroughly interrogated Robert Meriden the Third. We suspect Robert Meriden Senior may have been responsible for your grandfather's early passing. Robert Meriden the Second must have known or suspected this as well," explained Javier.

I guess they have been watching me closely.

"How did you arrive at this conclusion?" I asked.

"Before he took his own life back in 1946, Robert Meriden Senior lived in the tiny apartment above the garage in Warwick after his son Meriden the Second moved into the main house with his own family.

"My agents found a primitive prototype model of a what looks like a flying torpedo. It was made of metal and wood and was hanging from the ceiling in that apartment. It had 'G. Rossi 1917' inscribed on the bottom of it. We assumed that might have been what you were looking for. Is that why you were there, Mr. Rossi?"

This time I heard exactly what he said, clearly. I stared, smiling at the agent. I could not answer. I was, in fact, totally and utterly speechless.

Again the audience was on its feet going crazy as Diablo's lead singer Santiago completed their first set.

I could hardly contain myself either—what a night to remember!

57 THE JOURNEY CONTINUES

Four months after the concert, I was contacted by Homeland Security Agent Lt. Ojinaga to give a deposition relating to my verbal encounter with Robert Meriden in his garage in Warwick, Rhode Island. I complied with his request, but there was little information I could offer that would lend evidence to his case against Meriden.

Two more months passed, and the charge of attempted murder against Robert Meriden the Third had been dismissed due to "insufficient and unsubstantiated evidence." Lt. Ojinaga assured me he would bring up charges on Meriden again pending further investigation.

And although Meriden suspected and admitted *his* grandfather may have been directly involved with the death of Giuseppe Rossi and his daughter, he himself had no involvement.

As for charges against him of selling small arms, neither he nor his accomplices could be held due to the lack of any physical evidence. They were set free on their own personal recognizance, pending further investigation into the matter.

Nearly one year after that night at the concert, Lt. Ojinaga contacted me from his office in Boston. He stated that although they (Homeland Security) would need to hold my grandfather's prototype robot plane as evidence in their pending investigation against Meriden, we (my immediate family and relatives of Giuseppe Rossi) could view the prototype in a conference room in a federal building located in Boston if we so desired.

I requested pictures be sent to me of my grandfather's model; however, my request was denied due to the impending case against Robert Meriden the Third.

It had taken twenty years of my life to reach this juncture. The logistics of mobilizing family and relatives of Giuseppe Rossi for a fifteen-minute viewing of the device in Boston have been less fruitful. I look forward to the day I can place my hand on the model and see it firsthand.

Sadly, my dad and most of his brothers had passed by the time of this writing. But through the process of researching and writing, I have been able to reconnect with some of their children via e-mail correspondence. A family controversy seems to be brewing as to whether the model should be donated to the Smithsonian Institute in Washington or be kept in a local museum in Warwick, Rhode Island. My vote is keeping it local.

Finally, my wife, daughter, son, and I are doing well. Life is back to normal. That is to say, as "normal" a life can be with a rock star in the family, but then what fun is normal, after all?

Aaron Rossi
2012 Grammy Awards

Peter and Alecia (Rossi) Ojinaga

Jerry and Delia Rossi, 1950s

The Magnificent Seven
Nicholas, Michael, Augustino, Samuel
Gennaro, Lawrence, Antonio

Maria Angelina (Rossi) Stabile
On her wedding day

Giuseppe Rossi

Janet and Richard Rossi

RESOURCES

- The Pawtuxet Valley Preservation and Historical Society, 1679 Main Street, West Warwick, Rhode Island

- Diocese of Providence office of Catholic Cemeteries, 80 St. Mary's Drive, Cranston, Rhode Island

- Warwick, Rhode Island website: www.warwickri.gov/heritage/damatoshistory/pontiac21.htm

- Warwick City Clerk's Office, Warwick Rhode Island

- Sacred Heart Church, West Warwick, Rhode Island

- Department of the Air Force, United States Air Force Museum, 100 Spaatz St., Wright-Patterson Air Force Base, Ohio 45433-7102

- Victor Building built by Victor Evans in 1909—information supplied by Program Assistant CEROS/CAP, National Portrait Gallery, PO Box 37012, Victor Building, Suite 8300, MRC 973, Washing D.C. 20013-7012

- Kenneth P. Werrell, *The Evolution of the Cruise Missile* (1985).

- David Johnson, *V-1 V-2 Hitler's Vengeance On London* (Stein and Day, 1982).

- Mathias P. Harpin, *Trumpets In Jericho* (Commercial Printing and Publishing Co., 1961).

- Thomas Alvin Boyd, *Professional Amateur, The Biography of Charles Franklin Kettering* (Ayer Co. Pub, 1972).

- Michael J. Neufeld, *Von Braun, Dreamer of Space, Engineer of War* (Vintage, 2008).

- Arnold Green, *The Providence Plantations for Two Hundred And Fifty Years* (J.A. & R.A. Reid, Publishers and Printers, 1886).

- Ben Crawford, *Draper Loom Fixing* (Textile Industries, 1947).

- Leonard O. Warmer, "Robot Planes? A Natick man flew one in R.I. in 1918," *The Providence Sunday Journal*, June 1944.

- Josh Meyer, "Bush-era surveillance went beyond wire taps," *Los Angeles Times*, Saturday, July 11, 2009.

- John Kelly's Washington, Washingtonpost.com.

- Note: Many of the photographs came from postcards that were not dated or credited.

ABOUT THE AUTHOR

Richard B. Rossi was born on February 17, 1955, eighteen years to the day when his grandfather Giuseppe Rossi died. Since he was a boy, Richard has always been enchanted by his grandfather's vision and his persistence in bringing it to fruition. He was inspired to write *Patent for Murder* to bring late recognition to his grandfather and pay tribute to the Rossi family. Richard currently lives in Southern California and is exploring the notion of writing a second book, possibly a sequel to *Patent for Murder*.

Made in the USA
Lexington, KY
21 December 2012